FOR FELIX

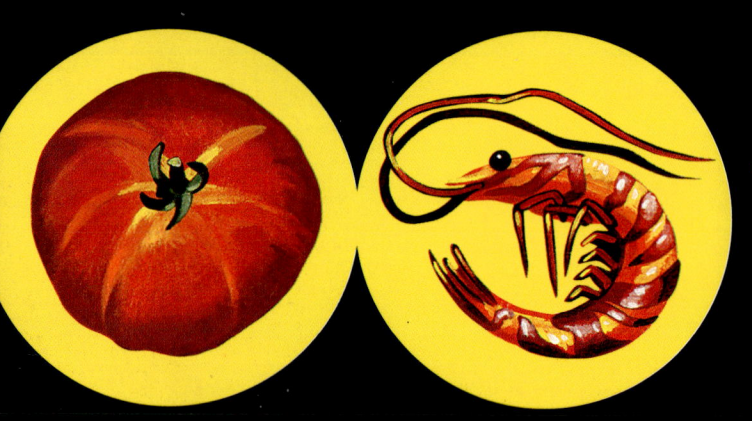

THECOSMICFEAST
DIVINE INSPIRATION FOR EARTHLY PLEASURES

DAVID McKAY ANNA JOHNSON KIRSTEN M

A William Heinemann Australia Book
published by Random House Australia Pty Ltd
20 Alfred Street, Milsons Point, NSW 2061
http://www.randomhouse.com.au

Sydney   New York   Toronto
London   Auckland   Johannesburg
and agencies throughout the world

First published 1997
Copyright © David McKay, Anna Johnson, Kirsten McKay

All rights reserved. No part of this publication may be reproduced, stored in a retrieval system, or transmitted in any form or by any means, electronic, mechanical, photocopying, recording or otherwise, without the prior written permission of the Publisher.

National Library of Australia
Cataloguing-in-Publication Data

McKay, David 1959-.
    The cosmic feast.

ISBN 0 09 183640 9

1. Astrology and diet. 2. Cookery I. Johnson, Anna, 1966-.
II. Title.
133.586415

Designed by Katie Christie, radiate design
Printed and Bound by
South China Printing Co. (1988) Ltd in
Hong Kong

10 9 8 7 6 5 4 3 2 1

contents

aries	**raw hide bbq**	**4**
taurus	**beyond yum cha**	**14**
gemini	**cocktail lounge**	**22**
cancer	**latin liason**	**32**
leo	**a regal indian feast**	**40**
virgo	**sunday brunch**	**52**
libra	**afternoon tea party**	**64**
scorpio	**pablo's passion**	**74**
sagittarius	**a game affair**	**82**
capricorn	**a traditional dinner**	**92**
aquarius	**picnic**	**102**
pisces	**midnight feast**	**110**

For many of us, astrology is a secret pleasure.   We find ourselves casting furtive glances over the horoscope pages of glossy magazines or secretly delving into the back pages of the newspaper for celestial guidance, all the while feigning disdain • The excesses of the hippy era have made astrology taboo, and the result is a kind of astrological neurosis. Maybe you're burning to ask someone the immortal words, What's your star sign?, but you're frightened that you'll sound like Barry White • Maybe you'd like to find your way into the thoughts and heart of a Scorpio, or simply seduce a Virgo?   Who are you going to call?   The psychic friends network? We don't think so.   Turn instead to The Cosmic Feast to find your way around Zodiac mindblocks • In the pages of this book we're outing astrology, and we're doing it with food.   Working through the Zodiac with tastes, aromas, textures, colours, music and wonderful ingredients, this book builds a portrait of the twelve sun signs through the five senses • Travelling way beyond the platitudes that are known to sum up each sign we go to the heart, and more importantly, the belly, of the issue • One might sense that Gemini is a restless soul but few know that the sign is utterly commitment phobic when it comes to three course sit down dinners.   One assumes that Scorpios have a passionate, kinky streak but who could guess that it is the pungent flavour of fermented fish sauce that they really crave?   Pisceans are positively passive aggressive about choosing from the menu, and Cancerians are heavily co-dependent on dairy products and shellfish • Such specifics when it comes to your would-be lover's palette might seem mystic at first.   Yet planting and harvesting by the cycle of the moon and seasons follows ancient codes • The links are sometimes uncanny.   Cancerians ruled by the Moon really do love pale foods, while nervous, skittish Air signs [Aquarius, Gemini, Libra] will flit around your buffet like quirky squirrels, and distractedly nibble at nutty, herby little snacks • Forget the suckling pig. Traditional, domesticated Earth signs [Taurus, Capricorn, Virgo] need food that's solid and pure. Forget concept dining. Fire signs [Aries, Leo, Sagittarius] are repelled by cold cuts and room temperature cheeses.   Light

begin

THE BELLY OF THE FEAST
A SPELL BOOK FOR THE MODERN CHEF

up the Weber instead.   And as for the squishy Water signs [Scorpio, Pisces, Cancer] they put mystery and romance on their weekly shopping lists right below wine and bread. So don't bore them with sliced ham and potato salad • To misquote a famous French architect - Love is in the details.   You've prepared the perfect food, so what about the context? Which touches will turn your lounge room into a lust zone? Consider the music.   Very seriously.   The generic Astrid Gilberto CD just isn't going to work for you. Aries wants something brand new.   Taurus wants to sing along. Gemini needs a staccatto back-beat to enhance the witty conversation, Cancer wants to be serenaded, and Leos are partial to pomp.   Virgo will probably bring their own music while Libra looks for the heavy swoon factor.   Arias and howling violins assuage the extreme desires of Scorpio, and Sagittarius is the only sign that honestly loves world music. Capricorn can be Baroque given half a chance, Aquarius needs electronic beeps, and Pisces purr for lyrical melancholy • The lighting must be just so.   One sign's candlelit feast is another's antiquated fiasco. Colour is as crucial as wine and the appropriate flowers unleash the mood faster than a falling star.   Don't panic.   Just turn to the glossary at the back • Dictating every detail from your choice of herbs to the texture of your pie crust, astrology is more than a party trick or a pin cushion for the barbs of sceptics.   In the hands of a sensualist the Zodiac is a garden of earthly delights where each sign blossoms with the correct touch • The Cosmic Feast says, forget the essential oils and ditch the complicated planetary alignment charts, go directly to the kitchen to weave your spell on the psyche and the senses.   It is at the dinner table that ideas are born, and, above all, love is ignited •

ARIES
raw hide barbecue

THE ARIES APPETITE

If you believed all the bad press that Mars, the ruling planet of Aries, received you'd think that this sign's motto was 'Make war not love!' Not quite. Beneath the volcanic surface of the aggro, sporty, sweaty, action-packed Aries personality is a romantic optimist. To release the schmaltz you must challenge them. Blowtorch their tastebuds with the force of garlic, chillies and spring onions, get mucho macho with a line of tequila shooters, then soothe their scorched senses with a jug of sangria. A Tex-Mex style barbecue suits Aries down to the gravel. As Mars is the red planet, Arian food looks fiery, even bloody. Whip the lamb off the Weber slightly raw at the centre, choose the richest orange pumpkins for the chilled soup, splash a little paprika over the avocado dressing and don't be shocked when your guest asks for double serves of sweet banana chillies. Aries are so fond of stimulant herbs that they expect to get a kick out of every course, that's why the guavas must be poached in cinnamon and vanilla. Forget comfort food. Another advantage of the barbecue is a certain proximity to the naked flame, broad daylight, and woodsmoke. Outdoorsy and informal, this spread flatters the Aries notion that they are ready for anything and utterly self-determined. Lazy guests? Hell no. Just let them grab the tongs and relight that there barbecue. At all costs avoid fuss. Ritualised formal courses, watery delicate ingredients and dimly lit cloistered interiors will have these cow pokes outta' there faster than you can mutter: 'Spaghetti Western'.

THE ARIES SEDUCTION

Vincent Van Gogh was an Aries and though he never got around to painting his birth flower - the daisy - there is a raw immediacy to his rich palette and speedy brushstrokes that combine adult passion and childlike impatience. If Vincent was coming for dinner you wouldn't stultify his spirits with cool jazz and brittle snackfood, would you? No way. Instead the Aries seduction works like an action painting - a jug of wine here, a wild dollop of avocado there, the whole scene splashed in sunlight and let the corn chips fall where they may. Don't fiddle with the details and serve it all up instead with broad strokes • The stimulant overload of the food [cayenne, roasted beast, booze, coffee] must be equalled, if not outdone, by the setting. Sprawl out on a bright red Navajo rug, serve the food on vivid hand-painted Tuscan plates and toast to the mad genius of Harry Houdini with sturdy tumblers. Forget the good crystal, Aries tend to slam things down to make their point • Pounding Cuban rhythms, Mexican love ballads and guitar rock are fine as background music but must never be louder than your ram. They want you to hear what they're saying, over and over. Conversationally Aries like to be wrestled and jousted but, ultimately, undefeated. This tryst is about ego massage. If you serve them the food they love, play them the music they love, and espouse the values they live by, they won't find you submissive. No, they'll just think you have great taste •

cheese & spring onion quesadillas with bowls of black olives **marinated barbecued leg of lamb** chillied pumpkin with walnuts wrapped in corn husks **roasted potatoes with avocado dressing** sweet banana chillies, barbecued with sour cream, coriander & chives **spiced lentil & spinach salad** fresh guavas poached in cinnamon & vanilla

drinks

tequilla shooters with spicy chasers [with the quesadillas and olives]
sangria mexicana [with the lamb & salads] **spiced coffee [with the guavas]**

cheese & spring onion quesadillas with bowls of black olives

1 tablespoon yoghurt
300 g cheddar cheese, grated
1/2 red capsicum, chopped
1/2 green capsicum, chopped
2 spring onions, chopped
6 flour tortillas
1 ripe avocado
2 tablespoons fresh coriander
zest of 1 lemon
salt and pepper

- Slice the avocado finely.
- Mix the grated cheese with the yoghurt, spring onions, diced capsicum, coriander leaves, lemon zest, salt and pepper.
- Spread the cheese mix onto the tortillas and lay the sliced avocado on top. Fold the tortilla in half and place in the refrigerator till needed - up to 4 hours.
- Lightly oil a flat frypan and place the tortillas in the oil. Cook over a medium heat till the outside of the tortillas are golden and crispy and the cheese is melted. They can be finished in the oven if necessary.
- Serve the quesadillas with bowls of black olives.

marinated barbecued leg of lamb

1 leg of lamb, boneless, rolled and tied
Chilli paste
12 dried chillis, seeded
6 cloves garlic, unpeeled
3 tablespoons cider vinegar
1/2 teaspoon toasted cumin seeds
1/2 teaspoon black peppercorns
1 teaspoon salt
2 teaspoons sugar

SAUCE
4 large tomatoes, skinned, seeded and chopped
1 small onion, finely chopped
1 teaspoon rosemary
3 tablespoons fresh coriander
Cayenne pepper to taste
2 limes, cut into quarters, for garnish
Chilli paste

- Chop the chillis into large pieces.
- Heat a large frypan and throw in the chillis. Toast them for a few minutes before covering in boiling water and leaving to seep for 30 minutes.
- Roast the garlic in a hot oven till darkened on the outside but still soft and mushy inside.
- Drain the chillis and, in a food processor, work the chilli flesh with the cider vinegar, roasted garlic, salt, sugar, cumin and 3/4 cup of water. Blend until smooth and divide into two lots, putting half to one side for final glazing.
- Rub the leg of lamb with the other half of the chilli paste and refrigerate for at least 3 or 4 hours.

COOKING THE LAMB
- Preheat oven to 220°C
- Place lamb in oven and cook for 20 minutes.
- Finish the lamb over a hot barbecue, basting as you go with the remaining chilli paste. This will take 15–20 minutes. The outside of the lamb should be very glazed and well cooked, the inside remaining pink. [If you prefer your lamb well done, add 10 minutes to the oven timing.]

SAUCE
- Sauté the onion with the rosemary till they are softened.
- Add the fresh tomato pulp and cook for 15–20 minutes over a slow heat. Once the tomatoes have softened to a cooked mass, turn off the heat.
- Sprinkle with salt and cayenne pepper. Fold in the chopped coriander leaves.

TO SERVE
- Slice the lamb and serve with the fresh tomato sauce. Garnish with fresh lime.

chillied pumpkin with walnuts wrapped in corn husks

1/2 pumpkin, skinned and seeded
2 large green chillis, seeded and chopped finely
1 onion, finely chopped
3 cloves garlic
2 handfuls walnuts, chopped
100 g butter
Corn husks [the outside leaves of a corn cob]

- Slice the pumpkin into fine wedges.
- Sauté the onion, chilli and garlic together in some olive oil. Add the chopped walnuts and set to one side.
- Lay some corn husks on a bench top, overlapping one another to form a star shape, and place the pumpkin in the centre. Place some of the walnut mixture on top of the pumpkin and add a large dob of butter.
- Fold in the sides of the husks so that you have a well-sealed packet. Tie the packet together with string to further secure them against falling apart when on the barbecue.
- Repeat this till you have 6 neat packets.
- Place on a hot barbecue and turn occasionally for 35 minutes.
- Serve with the lamb.

roasted potatoes with avocado dressing

1 kg chat potatoes
1/2 ripe avocado, peeled
Juice of one lime
11/2 tablespoons cider vinegar
2 tablespoons fresh coriander, chopped
1 clove garlic, finely minced
2/3 cup olive oil
1 large egg yolk
Salt and pepper
Green top of 1 shallot, finely sliced
2 tablespoons sour cream

- Roast the potatoes with olive oil, salt and pepper.

AVOCADO DRESSING
- Combine the avocado, lime juice, vinegar, coriander, garlic and oil in a blender. Process until puréed.
- In a bowl, place the egg yolk and whisk slightly. Then, slowly whisk in the avocado mixture. Don't do this too quickly or it will separate.
- Once all the mixture has been incorporated, season well and mix in the chopped shallot and sour cream.
- Serve on the side of the roasted potatoes.

sweet banana chillies, barbecued with sour cream, coriander & chives

6 red sweet banana chillis
Olive oil
Juice of 2 limes
250 ml sour cream
2 tablespoons fresh coriander, chopped
2 tablespoons chives, chopped

- Brush the banana chillis with olive oil and chargrill on the barbecue till the flesh is soft and moist.
- Allow to cool.
- When cool enough to handle, slit lengthways and spoon in the sour cream.
- Garnish with the chives and coriander, and sprinkle with lime juice.

spiced lentil & spinach salad

450 g puy lentils, picked over for stones and rinsed
1 bunch English spinach, stalks removed and washed
2 large onions, chopped
5 cloves garlic, chopped
2 tablespoons ground cumin
4 tablespoons olive oil
Juice of 2 lemons
Salt and pepper

- Cover the lentils with cold water. Bring to the boil and simmer gently for 10-15 minutes. Drain and refresh with cold water.
- In a large frypan, sauté the onion and garlic with the cumin in 1 tablespoon of olive oil. Once the onion has softened, throw in the spinach and cook quickly, until it has wilted.
- Remove from the heat and combine in a salad bowl with the lentils, olive oil and lemon juice.
- Season well with salt and pepper.

fresh guavas poached in cinnamon & vanilla

6 fresh guavas
200 g sugar
2 cinnamon sticks
1 vanilla bean, split lengthways
5 cloves
2 bay leaves
Zest of 1 lime
500 ml water

- Make the syrup with all of the ingredients except the guavas. Bring to the boil and simmer gently for 15 minutes.
- Peel the guavas, cut in half and remove the seeds.
- Place the fruit into the boiling syrup and poach gently till it has softened but still holds its shape.
- Remove the fruit from the syrup with a slotted spoon and set to one side while the syrup continues to reduce.
- When the syrup is thick and syrupy, pour it onto the guavas and allow to cool before serving.
- Serve with freshly whipped, sweetened cream, sprinkled with cinnamon and cocoa.

tequilla shooters with spicy chasers

250 ml tequilla
Juice of 2 limes
Salt
Sangria [spicy chaser]
1/2 cup fresh orange juice
1/4 cup tomato juice
1/4 cup fresh lime juice
4 teaspoons grenadine syrup
1/4 teaspoon salt
1/4 teaspoon salsa picante [tabasco sauce]

- Mix all the sangria ingredients together in a jug and refrigerate for at least one hour before serving.
- Pour the sangria into 6 shot glasses.
- Dip the rim of another 6 shot glasses into lime juice and then into the salt. Pour the tequilla into the glasses.
- Each person drinks the tequilla, followed by the sangria.

sangria mexicana

1 cup fresh lime juice
1/2 cup sugar
1 bottle red wine
250 ml sparkling mineral water
Fresh lime slices, for garnish

- Mix all ingredients together in a jug.
- Pour into tall glasses over ice cubes and garnish with fresh lime.

spiced coffee

1 pot hot plunger coffee
2 cinnamon sticks
1/2 dozen fennel seeds
100 g brown sugar

- Combine all the ingredients and allow to sit for 5 minutes before serving.

TAURUS
beyond yum cha

THE TAUREAN APPETITE

Some people act like their sign and others just look like it. Taurus is the bull. Bulls have deep broad nostrils and rather dark, penetrating eyes. Have a look at Henry Fonda, Bono, Salvador Dali, Ricky Nelson, Karl Marx and Rudolph Valentino, then think about their nostrils. So dark! So cavernous! They compete only with the pitch-black pupils for attention. Known as the song birds of the zodiac, Taurus girls also have that nostril thing happening - witness Ella Fitzgerald in action, and Debbie Harry's pouting pixie nose. Or better still, watch Barbra Streisand in loving close-up. As she spirals out into an apoplexy of emotion, home in on the nostrils. First they inhale with incredible drama, shrinking into her nose like the nestled wings of a frightened bird and then majestically they unfurl - spreading, soaring, taking flight in a full-flared catharsis. To kill the theory there are pinched nosed Taureans, the perfectly chiselled Rod McKuen for example or the bony snouted Michelle Pfeiffer. But what the nostrils mean, what they are pointing towards, is a very obvious, pronounced sensuality. Governed by Venus the planet of love, Amazons and full-blown roses, Taurus is the bull in the china shop. They are earthy and aesthetic, touchy, feely, thirsty, hungry and blatantly horny. Food is an expression of domestic security [the home paddock] and an aphrodisiac. Grazing across the Chinese banquet Taurus needs to feel secure to feel roused - that means solid meaty textures with rich flavours such as prawns, lobsters, chicken and beef, accented by ambrosial seasonings like coriander, peppermint and the nostril-twitching sweetness of jasmine rice. Flowers and perfumed fruits, and creamy coconut custards round off the experience. This is not the sign of the diet or the meal on the run, instead it is blue ribbon pampering for an appetite as solid as an ox and a sense of smell as deep as Barry White's dulcet baritone.

THE TAUREAN SEDUCTION

It's all a bit Bornhoffen for the Taurus. Haystacks replete with wenches or stablehands, rolling cornfields, orchards and sweet-scented gardens are the open-air boudoirs of their dreams, but there is also a subtle side to bullish tastes. Out of the barn and into the penthouse they respond to lush upholstery and contemporary art. Fuse The Beverly Hillbillies with Architectural Digest and you get the picture. Taurus, in the words of the poets Osmond, are a little bit country and a little bit rock and roll. While you lay the table with hearty fare don't forget to orchestrate the evening's soundtrack. Without music the seduction is dead and the bull walks. As they relentlessly forage from venison to rabbit you must swing like a metronome from one inspired Taurus love song to the next. Tammy Wynette, Dame Nellie Melba, Enya, Janet Jackson, Roy Orbison, James Brown, Eric Burdon, Stevie Wonder, Burt Bacharach and even Barnesy can form your seduction compilation, just rush them onto the stereo without stopping to look at the nostrils on each CD cover ■ Sounds, smells, textures dealt with, it's time to move onto the visuals. Taureans aren't into monochrome or animal prints. Set the table instead with delicate eastern ceramics the colours of spring - celadon green, pale pink and china blue - and arrange generous vases of poppies, columbines, foxgloves and pink roses. After this concerted effort Taurus, unlike Gemini or Sagittarius, will not expect a fiesty argument or an oratory performance. While they graze sweetly you can hand them a post-feast whisky and expire from the strain of creating such a bower of felicity. Sit back, recoup and then watch the nostrils of your beloved. Once they start to flare, anticipate the ultimate rewards of a Taurus seduction when the dozing beast of sensuality rouses and transforms into raging bull ■

deep fried prawn balls with a sweet chilli & cucumber dipping sauce lobster & mixed fungi salad with egg noodles **brisket of beef with red braised sauce & spinach** chilli roasted chicken with deep-fried cabbage & spring onion **jasmine rice** ginger & coconut milk custards with fresh mango salad

champagne [to start] **sauvignon blanc** jasmine tea **fortified muscatel**

drinks

deep fried prawn balls with a sweet chilli & cucumber dipping sauce

PRAWN BALLS
500 g prawn meat [green]
1/4 teaspoon grated ginger
2 tablespoons spring onion, chopped
1 clove garlic, chopped finely
2 coriander stalks, chopped finely
1 whole egg
2 drops sesame oil

DIPPING SAUCE
2 tablespoons sugar
2 tablespoons rice vinegar
2 tablespoons grated ginger
2 tablespoons light soy
1 red chilli, seeded and chopped finely
1 shallot, finely chopped
1 Lebanese cucumber, sliced very finely

- Place the prawn meat, ginger and garlic in a food processor. Process till it forms a ball. Add egg and remaining ingredients. Process till all ingredients are well combined. Season well.
- With a damp teaspoon, shape prawn balls and place onto a plate that has been covered with cling film.
- Gently drop balls into hot oil. Cook for a few minutes. Remove from the oil and drain on absorbent paper.
- Serve with dipping sauce and garnish with fresh coriander.

DIPPING SAUCE
- Slice the cucumber, sprinkle with salt and drain in a colander for 30 minutes. Wash and pat dry. Combine all other ingredients and add cucumber when ready to serve.

lobster & fresh mixed fungi salad with egg noodles

2 medium-sized cooked lobsters, meat removed from shell and claws
1 punnet Enoki mushrooms
1 punnet oyster mushrooms
1 punnet fresh black wood fungus
180 g fresh egg noodles, blanched [dried will do]
1 celery stalk, julienned

SAUCE
3 heaped tablespoons palm sugar
2 tablespoons oyster sauce
30 ml light soy sauce
1 teaspoon freshly grated ginger
100 ml peanut oil
150 ml water
Freshly ground black pepper
Juice of 1 lemon

SAUCE
- Put the water and the sugar together in a small saucepan. Bring to the boil and continue to simmer for 5 minutes. Add the ginger, soy and oyster sauce and finally, the peanut oil.
- Remove from heat and add the lemon juice.

TO ASSEMBLE
- Combine the noodles and the three wild fungi with the celery. Add half of the sauce and toss well. Place on a plate in a mound. Slice the lobster meat and place attractively on top of the noodles. Spoon over more of the sauce and cracked pepper and serve.
- Should be served at room temperature.

beef brisket with red braised sauce & spinach

1 1/2 kg brisket of beef
Chicken stock to cover beef
350 ml Shaohung wine
1 large piece ginger
5 star anise
2 sticks cinnamon
6 cloves garlic
150 ml soy sauce
Zest of 1 orange
6 dried shitake mushrooms
150 g brown sugar
1 teaspoon sesame oil
1 tablespoon peanut oil
1 bunch english spinach

- Seal beef well on both sides. Place in large stockpot, cover with chicken stock and bring to boil. Reduce heat and skim surface well to remove all scum.
- After 20 minutes add next nine ingredients. Simmer gently for approximately 1 1/2 hours or until beef is tender.
- Remove from heat, cool in stock. Refrigerate overnight.
- Next day, remove all the fat on top and reheat beef.
- Remove from the liquid and keep warm. Reduce the sauce.

TO FINISH
- In a wok heat 1 tablespoon of peanut oil and sesame oil till hot. Add the cleaned and trimmed spinach. Stirfry quickly adding 1 ladle of sauce.

TO SERVE
- Place the spinach onto a platter, slice the beef and lay on top of the spinach. Spoon over the sauce.

chilli roasted chicken with deep-fried cabbage & spring onion

CHICKEN
9 chicken thigh fillets [skin off]
2 teaspoons ground black pepper
1 tablespoon chilli sambal
2 tablespoons kecap manis [sweet soy]
1 tablespoon peanut oil

CABBAGE
1/2 chinese cabbage
Vegetable oil for deep frying
1 tablespoon toasted sesame seeds
1 tablespoon castor sugar
1/2 teaspoon salt
1 bunch spring onions
100 ml reduced chicken stock

TO PREPARE CHICKEN
- Combine all the ingredients and mix in thoroughly with the chicken thighs. Allow to marinate for at least 2 hours.

TO PREPARE CABBAGE
- Shred the cabbage very finely. Heat the oil till hot and deep fry for 2 minutes. Take out of oil and drain on absorbent paper. Sprinkle with sesame seeds, salt and sugar.

TO COOK THE CHICKEN
- Place chicken in an oven dish. Cook in moderate oven for about 20 minutes. Remove the chicken and set to one side. Add chicken stock and spring onions to the chicken pan, swirl well to collect all the pieces. Pour sauce over the chicken and top with deep-fried cabbage. Sprinkle with sesame oil and coriander.

ginger & coconut milk custards with fresh mango salad

3 tablespoons grated ginger
150 ml cream
300 ml coconut milk
8 egg yolks
2 whole eggs
100 ml castor sugar
2 ripe mangoes
Coconut, roasted and shaved for garnish

- Bring the cream, coconut milk and ginger to just below boiling. Do not boil.
- In a bowl combine the egg yolks, whole eggs and sugar, whisk well and gradually add the coconut milk mix. Stir together and pass through a fine sieve.
- Pour the custard mixture into 6 custard moulds right to the top. Place into a bain-marie and fill to half way with hot water [not boiling]. Cover with foil and bake in a low oven 125°C for 30–35 minutes.
- Remove from bain-marie and allow to cool before serving.
- Serve with sliced mango and toasted coconut.

cocktail lounge gemini

THE GEMINI APPETITE

Geminis are a bit like French intellectuals. They like to consider the body as a map, desire as a compass governed by the mind, the senses as a train journey - with each sight, taste and texture a brief stop - and a meal as a conversation prone to constant tangents and divergences. In a phrase - it's brain sex. Skittish, sophisticated, impatient, urbane and mobile, this is the sign of poets, politicians and old queens. A pot roast and Albinoni are not going to do it for them and neither will laborious haute cuisine. Instead of slaving over a soufflé or nursing a complex tagine, you'd be better off hiring some good caterers and reading five Booker Prize novels instead. Short, fast, brilliant anecdotes served with quick, light luscious snacks. Get it? Got it? Good. Piquant green flavours like dill, fennel, fenugreek and parsley delight the predominantly herby Gemini palette. The lighter tastes of domestic fowl - chicken, turkey and goose - brought down to earth with rich fruit accents of apricots and peaches, subtly balance the constantly darting Mercurial mind. Flitting as they do between the physical world and the mental, the role of food for Gemini is to build a sensual bridge between the two. Sprinkle rosemary into their palmiers, sneak fennel seed into the mayonnaise, serve up constant variety [French, Japanese, Meditteranean] and invent a theory to go with each. Prepare these foods knowing that rosemary calms the stomach and the central nervous system, but never ever couch your menu in those terms. Dullsville! Instead, tell a Gemini that the crudités and little munchy things are a theoretical tribute to the Cartesian dialectic of the mind/body split. The way to their heart is through their brains, that's where all the digestion is happening.

THE GEMINI SEDUCTION

Reverse everything thing you've heard about the laws of seduction for Gemini. Forget two people alone on a Saturday night, candlelight, gentle vibes and the phone off the hook. Such a demand for undivided attention and the sheer weight of romantic cliché will repulse your prey. So, Wednesday night, a cocktail party stuffed to the gills with glittering, bizarre guests, divine sophisto-cat finger food [celeriac and smoked salmon remoulade, fabulous], nervous staccato jazz in the background or even better a smattering of performance poets having haiku outbursts [remember the TV attention span] and no time spent dawdling near the stove. Mercury aesthetics are rather clean and crisp with shades of clear yellow, greens, blues and shimmery silver. I didn't say tinsel. A Calder mobile or a darting paper plane enclosing an obtuse message aimed right at them should grab their attention. But only for a second. If you can get a Gemini to sit down at a dinner table, congrats. To keep them there consider beautiful diversions. Butcher's paper with crayons or a calico tablecloth screen printed in silver ink with Cole Porter lyrics [so clever!], tiny white flowers frozen inside the ice cubes or a setting created like a mirror image: two carafes, four champagne flutes, two identical candles, two pepper mills, two pithy compliments where one would do ■ At all costs avoid the static. Duck, weave and when you're both finally alone ensnare with lively diversions - a fairy trail of Herald Tribunes and this month's New Yorker placed on little coffee tables that lead to the bedroom, the windows left open permitting Hitchcock views of the neighbours, and a slightly distracted air as you answer the phone with one hand and open the champagne with the other. Geminis must be outstripped at their own game, outdazzled, out-delighted but never overstuffed! Let wit be the food of love and chic nibblies subtly fuel the furnace ■

fresh prawns with a fennel seed & dill mayonnaise marinated chicken with a spicy tomato & apricot chutney **crudités with a spinach, hazelnut & olive oil dipping sauce** celeriac & smoked salmon remoulade served on garlic croûtes **vegetable rolls in rice paper with soy dipping sauce** mushroom, rosemary & almond palmiers **chicken liver mousse with warm toast**

champagne, champagne & more champagne **drinks**

fresh prawns with a fennel seed & dill mayonnaise

1 kg cooked prawns
1 cup very good mayonnaise
1 teaspoon roasted fennel seeds, crushed
1/2 bunch fresh dill, chopped
1 lemon
Cracked black pepper

- Peel the prawns, leaving the tail on.
- Combine all other ingredients in a bowl and store in the refrigerator till needed. Serve prawns with mayonnaise in a bowl, with wedges of lemon for garnish.

marinated chicken with a spicy tomato & apricot chutney

CHICKEN
10 chicken thigh fillets
2 cloves garlic, chopped
1 teaspoon grated ginger
3 tablespoons olive oil
1 tablespoon curry powder

CHUTNEY
1 kg ripe tomatoes, peeled and chopped
500 g chopped fresh apricots
2 medium onions chopped
1 cup brown sugar [solidly packed]
3/4 cup currants
2 cloves garlic, chopped
1/2 teaspoon dry mustard
1/4 teaspoon chilli powder
2 teaspoons strong curry powder
2 teaspoons ground allspice
1 1/2 cups brown vinegar

CHICKEN
- Cut chicken into bite-size pieces and marinate with the other ingredients for at least 1 hour.
- Grill the chicken pieces on a high heat for a few minutes.
- Serve warm with the tomato and apricot chutney. Garnish with fresh chopped coriander.

CHUTNEY
- Combine all ingredients in a large pot, stir over heat till the sugar is dissolved. Bring to boil and simmer for about 1 hour until the mixture has thickened. Pour into sterilised jars and seal when cold.

crudités with a spinach, hazelnut & olive oil dipping sauce

Selection of fresh
vegetables to include:
Crisp fennel
Asparagus
Green runner beans
Celery stalks
Baby sweet corn
Cauliflower flowerets
Baby carrots
Cherry tomatoes

DIPPING SAUCE
1 bunch English spinach
1 handful roasted hazelnuts
150 ml olive oil
Salt and pepper
10 fresh basil leaves
1 tablespoon Dijon mustard
Juice 1 lemon

- Bring a pot of water to the boil. Pick over the spinach removing stalks and any bruised pieces. Blanch the spinach and then immediately refresh it under cold running water.
- Once the spinach is cold, squeeze it in your hands to remove any excess liquid.
- In a food processor, place the mustard, hazelnuts, salt, pepper and lemon juice. Process for a few moments until the hazelnuts are quite fine and then add the spinach and basil. Process once again till a ball has formed. Leaving the processor running, gradually add the olive oil until a smooth, running dipping sauce is achieved.
- Serve at room temperature with the fresh crudités.

celeriac & smoked salmon remoulade served on garlic croûtes

1 French bread stick
Olive oil
1 bulb celeriac
Juice of 1 lemon
1/2 cup very good mayonnaise
1 teaspoon Dijon mustard
1 teaspoon grated horseradish
1 tablespoon chopped parsley
100 g smoked salmon
1 clove garlic, crushed

- Add the crushed garlic to the olive oil and leave, to flavour the oil, for at least one hour.
- Slice the bread stick into 1 cm thick slices, lay on a flat baking tray and brush each piece lightly with the garlic and olive oil. Toast in the oven till the bread crisp. This can be done a day in advance.
- Peel the celeriac and place in acidulated water [water with juice of 1 lemon]. Shred the celeriac using a shredding disc on your food processor.
- Chop the smoked salmon into fine julienne.
- In a bowl, combine the mayonnaise with the Dijon mustard and horseradish. Add the shredded celeriac and smoked salmon. Mix through well and finish with cracked black pepper and parsley.
- Just before required, spoon the remoulade onto the croûtes and serve.

vegetable rolls in rice paper with soy dipping sauce

VEGETABLE ROLLS

1 carrot, finely julienned
1 stick celery, finely julienned
4 green shallots, cut in quarters lengthways
1 small red capsicum, finely julienned
1/2 Chinese cabbage, shredded finely
1/2 teaspoon grated ginger
2 cloves garlic, minced
1 tablespoon kecap manis [sweet soy]
1/2 bunch chopped coriander
1 tablespoon desiccated coconut, toasted
2 tablespoons peanut oil
18 sheets Thai rice paper [15–17 cm]

DIPPING SAUCE

1/2 cup light soy sauce
1 tablespoon plum sauce
1/2 teaspoon grated ginger
2 teaspoons chopped coriander stalks
1 teaspoon toasted sesame seeds

VEGETABLE ROLLS

- Heat the peanut oil in a wok, add the garlic and ginger, followed by the carrot, celery, capsicum and coconut. Stirfry till softened [but still crunchy]. Add the cabbage, soy sauce and finely chopped coriander. Remove from heat and let it cool before rolling in the rice paper.

TO ASSEMBLE

- Cut each piece of rice paper in half. You will need a bowl of water to pass the rice paper through to soften it. It is best to do this one at a time.
- Lay the softened rice paper on a clean cloth and top with a spoonful of vegetable mix, fold in the long side to cover edge of mix, then roll up the narrow sides. Refrigerate till required.
- Just before serving, place the rolls in a steamer in a single layer, and steam covered with a lid. Serve hot with the dipping sauce.

DIPPING SAUCE

- Combine all the ingredients together in a bowl and mix thoroughly. Store in refrigerator till needed. Can be kept up to one week.

mushroom, rosemary & almond palmiers

375 g frozen puff pastry
1 egg, lightly beaten

FOR THE FILLING
250 g button mushrooms, sliced finely
2 cloves garlic, minced
4 shallots, chopped finely
1 good handful chopped almonds, toasted
1 tablespoon vegetable oil
1 onion, chopped very finely
1 handful grated parmesan cheese
1 teaspoon chopped rosemary
Salt and pepper
1 tablespoon butter

- Heat the oil and butter in a pan, add the garlic, rosemary and onion, stirring until the onion has softened. Add the sliced mushrooms and cook for a further 4–5 minutes. Stir in the chopped almonds and shallots. Season well with salt and pepper. Continue cooking for 1 more minute.
- Take off the heat and stir in the parmesan cheese.
- Place the mixture in a colander to drain away excess moisture. Set to one side till ready to assemble.

TO ASSEMBLE
- Roll the pastry on a lightly floured surface to a 25 cm by 35 cm rectangle. Cut this in half lengthways making two rectangles.
- Spread 1/2 mixture over 1 rectangle and repeat with the remaining mixture on the other rectangle.
- Fold in one long side of the rectangle to the centre of the mixture, brush the pastry with the egg and fold in the other side. Brush with more egg and fold in half along the seam of the join. Press down gently and refrigerate for 1 hour before cooking.

TO COOK
- Cut the rolls into 1 cm slices. Place these on a baking tray with the cut side upwards. Brush again with egg and bake in a moderate oven for about 10-15 minutes. Transfer to serving plate and serve warm.

chicken liver mousse with warm toast

500 g chicken livers
100 g butter
2 sprigs thyme, stalks removed
1 tablespoon sweet sherry or cognac
300 ml cream
1 loaf wholemeal bread
6 cornichon [baby gherkins]
Ground black pepper
Salt

- Clean the chicken livers very well ensuring that any greenish specks have been thoroughly removed. Pat the livers dry and set to one side.
- In a large frypan, melt half the butter. When it has melted, add half the chicken livers and half the thyme. Sauté in the butter till they are cooked but still pink in the centre.
- Remove the livers from the pan and place in a colander to drain. Repeat this process for the remaining livers.
- Once you have cooked the second batch of livers, return the pan to the heat and add the sherry and swivel around to pick up all the pieces of liver stuck to the pan. Turn off heat and reserve this liquor.
- Place livers in a food processor and process with the liquor until smooth. Pass the mixture through a fine sieve and season this purée very well with salt and pepper.
- In another bowl, whip the cream to soft peaks. Fold this into the liver purée and cover well with cling film and refrigerate till required. Serve on warm wholemeal toast, garnished with a slice of cornichon.

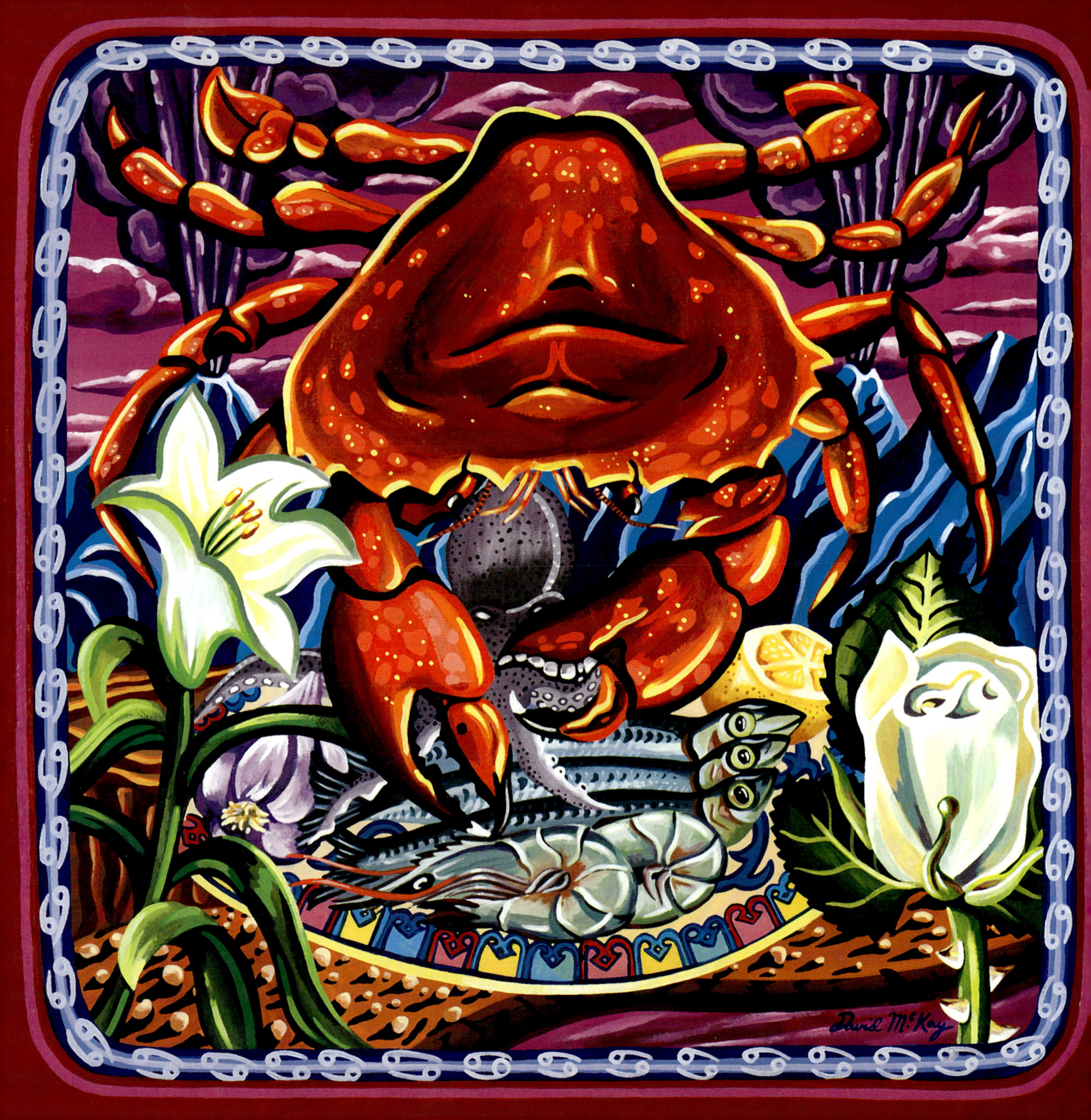
David McKay

cancer latin liason

THE CANCER APPETITE

Although Cancer's symbolic creature is the crab, cancer types are more soft centred than hard shelled. These are the refined homebodies of the zodiac who treat the kitchen as a high altar of the senses • Ruled by the moon, their foods are pale and pearly - leeks, lettuces, marrows, parsnips, turnips, rice, dairy products, seafood, shellfish, chocolate, spring water and white wine. Given such a broad and delectable palette it is easy to satisfy the Cancerian desire for filling, wholesome fare. A Spanish table of crunchy grilled sardines poised on dainty parsnip and potato cakes [spiced up with watercress and shallot salsa], followed by a rich Catalan casserole evokes tradition and the hearth. The dessert, a large round lemon and honey cheesecake pays obvious homage to the maternal bosom of Diana, the harvest goddess • Unlike tearaway Sagittarians or rebellious Scorpio, Cancerians are the poets of the kitchen. In their eyes every chipped plate, marble chopping board and yellowed recipe is a touchstone of warmth and creativity. Tell them the meal is a 200-year-old family recipe and let your cheeks grow flushed with emotion as you stir the pot, this is the sign of SNAGs, earth mothers, full moons and full bellies •

THE CANCER SEDUCTION

Cancer has been accused of being domestically obsessed, last seen roaming homewear stores and chefs' supply warehouses with glassy possum eyes. To keep this warm, fuzzy feeling alive you must polish your lair like the glowing interior of a pearl. Cancer aesthetics are white-washed, and silvery, perhaps a little bit Norwegian. Candles or accordion-pleated round paper lanterns should light the room softly, evocative instrumentals, 19th century Spanish guitar and a smattering of romantic piano must filter into the kitchen. Milky petalled flowers like lilies, acanthus, white geraniums and field roses scent the night air and float against a tablecloth of ivory raw silk. **As exquisite as your table may be, prepare for the fact that the real seduction of a Cancerian happens over the bench top. Try sleeping in your kitchen for a few nights before the dinner to heat up the vibe and dot the room with objects of anecdotal importance. Without seeming too calculated, investigate the proportions and strength of your kitchen table. Will it support the body weight of two wrestlers? I hope so.** As pre-dinner preamble feel free to tell family stories [this is the only sign in the zodiac who won't yawn] and even break out the photo albums. Go wild with everything domestic - aprons, hand-sewn table napkins encased in silver napkin rings, gleaming stainless steel equipment. One final little hint. As Cancer rules the stomach, it may pay to discreetly monitor the serving sizes, remember all those nursery rhymes about golden eggs and Jack Sprat - don't overstuff your goose!

grilled sardines on crisped parsnip & potato cakes with a watercress & shallot salsa mar i muntanya [catalan casserole of chicken, balmain bugs, prawns & squid] **majorcan style citrus & honey cheesecake**

drinks spanish cava [champagne] a spanish muscatel or an australian fruity riesling cremat

grilled sardines on crisped parsnip & potato cakes with watercress & shallot salsa

SARDINES
18 sardines

PARSNIP AND POTATO CAKES
3 parsnips
3 large potatoes
2 whole eggs
Salt and pepper
1/2 brown onion
1 tablespoon olive oil
Vegetable oil for cooking

WATERCRESS AND SHALLOT SALSA
3 shallots, chopped very finely
1/2 bunch watercress, cleaned, washed and dried
1 Lemon, zest and juice
1/2 head garlic, roasted and skins removed
1 teaspoon red wine vinegar
3 tablespoons olive oil
1 tomato, seeded and diced very finely
Pinch of cayenne pepper
1/2 small red capsicum, diced very finely

SARDINES
- On a flat baking tray lay the sardines down flesh to the tray. Lightly brush with olive oil and flash under the grill for approximately 1 minute - they cook very quickly under a hot grill.

PARSNIP AND POTATO CAKES
- Peel and grate the potatoes, parsnips and onion.
- Beat the eggs into the salt and pepper and the olive oil.
- Squeeze the potato and parsnip mixture very well to remove any excess moisture.
- Add the eggs and oil to the potato and mix through thoroughly.
- Just before serving, heat the vegetable oil till hot, drop in a large tablespoon of mixture and flatten it out to form a circle. Cook evenly on both sides and drain onto a paper towel. Make 18 [3 per person].

WATERCRESS AND SHALLOT SALSA
- In a bowl combine all the ingredients apart from the watercress. Mix together very well and set to one side.
- The watercress should have all the large stalks removed so all that remains are the leaves.
- Chop the cress finely and add this to the salsa.
- Allow to stand for at least 2 hours before serving.

TO SERVE
- Place the 3 crisp potato cakes onto each person's plate. Lay a grilled sardine on top and then finish with a teaspoon of salsa. Lemon wedges can be served on the side.

mar i muntanya / sea & mountain
[catalan casserole of chicken, balmain bugs, prawns & squid]

CASSEROLE
12 large green prawns
6 Balmain bugs [green]
6 small squid, cleaned and skinned
12-18 mussels, cleaned and debearded
3 cups strong fish stock
1 large chicken, cut into 6 pieces
2 onions, chopped
4 ripe tomatoes, peeled, seeded and chopped
4 cloves of garlic
6 threads saffron
3 sprigs thyme
1/2 cup dry white wine
1/2 cup dry sherry
Dash of Pernod

PICADA
2 cloves garlic
20 almonds, skinned and roasted
20 Hazelnuts, skinned and roasted
2 slices bread, fried in olive oil [crusts removed]
1/2 teaspoon salt
3 sprigs parsley
40 g cooking chocolate

- In a large pot, steam open the mussels in 1/2 an inch of white wine. Remove mussels from the liquid and set both to one side.
- In a heavy bottomed casserole dish sauté the onions, garlic and thyme for a few minutes in some olive oil, add the saffron threads and the white wine, simmer for a couple of minutes before adding the chopped tomatoes and the fish stock. Reduce to low heat continue cooking.
- Meanwhile, in another pan, sauté the pieces of chicken in olive oil on both sides till nice and golden. Remove from the oil and add to the tomato sauce and continue to simmer gently.
- In the same pan, sauté the green prawns and Balmain bugs till they turn pink. Remove and set to one side.
- Now sauté the squid, adding a little more oil if necessary. Set these to one side also. While the pan is still on the heat, pour in the sherry and with a wooden spoon, scrape along the bottom and the sides to collect all the bits and pieces stuck there. Now add this liquid to the tomato and chicken.
- The chicken should be almost ready by now, so turn off the heat and cover pan with a lid till almost ready.

TO MAKE THE PICADA
- This should really be made in a mortar and pestle, not a food processor. Into the mortar, place the garlic, almonds, hazelnuts, fried bread and chocolate. Crush all the ingredients and then add the chopped parsley. Add enough oil to just cover the ingredients and then slowly work the oil into the mixture to form a thick paste.
- 5 minutes before serving, add the picada and the pernod to the chicken and stir them in gently. Then the squid and any juices, then the prawns and juices, finishing with the mussels, just enough to warm them through.
- Serve with boiled rice and a tomato and green salad.

majorcan style citrus & honey cheesecake

1 cup hazelnuts
1/3 cup sugar
1/2 teaspoon ground cinnamon
70 g unsalted butter, melted
1 cup almonds

FILLING
750 g cream cheese, soft at room temperature
100 g sour cream
250 g honey
6 eggs
1 tablespoon lemon zest
1 tablespoon orange zest
1 teaspoon vanilla
60 g sugar
3 oranges, for garnish
100 ml cream for whipping

- To make the crust, chop the nuts and add to the sugar and cinnamon in a food processor. Add melted butter so that the mixture holds together. Press into the base of a spring-form tin. Set to one side. Preheat oven 180°C.
- Place the cream cheese and sour cream into bowl. Beat till smooth. Add honey and beat till all lumps are removed. Add egg yolks, fruit zest and vanilla. Mix in thoroughly.
- In a large bowl, whip the egg whites till soft, gradually beat in the sugar and continue beating to form stiff peaks. Fold whites into the cheese mixture and pour into the prepared cake tin. Bake in the oven on the middle rack for 45 minutes. Turn off the oven and leave to cool in the oven with the door ajar.
- Serve with sliced oranges and whipped cream.

cremat

1 cup brandy
11/2 cups rum
3 tablespoons castor sugar
2 sticks cinnamon
Peel of 1 lemon
Peel of 1 orange
4–6 cups strong black coffee [hot]
Candied orange peel dipped in chocolate

- In a saucepan combine all the ingredients except the coffee and candied orange peel.
- Warm the mixture gently, then ignite it and watch it flame up, then pour in the hot coffee. Serve immediately with candied orange peel dipped in chocolate.

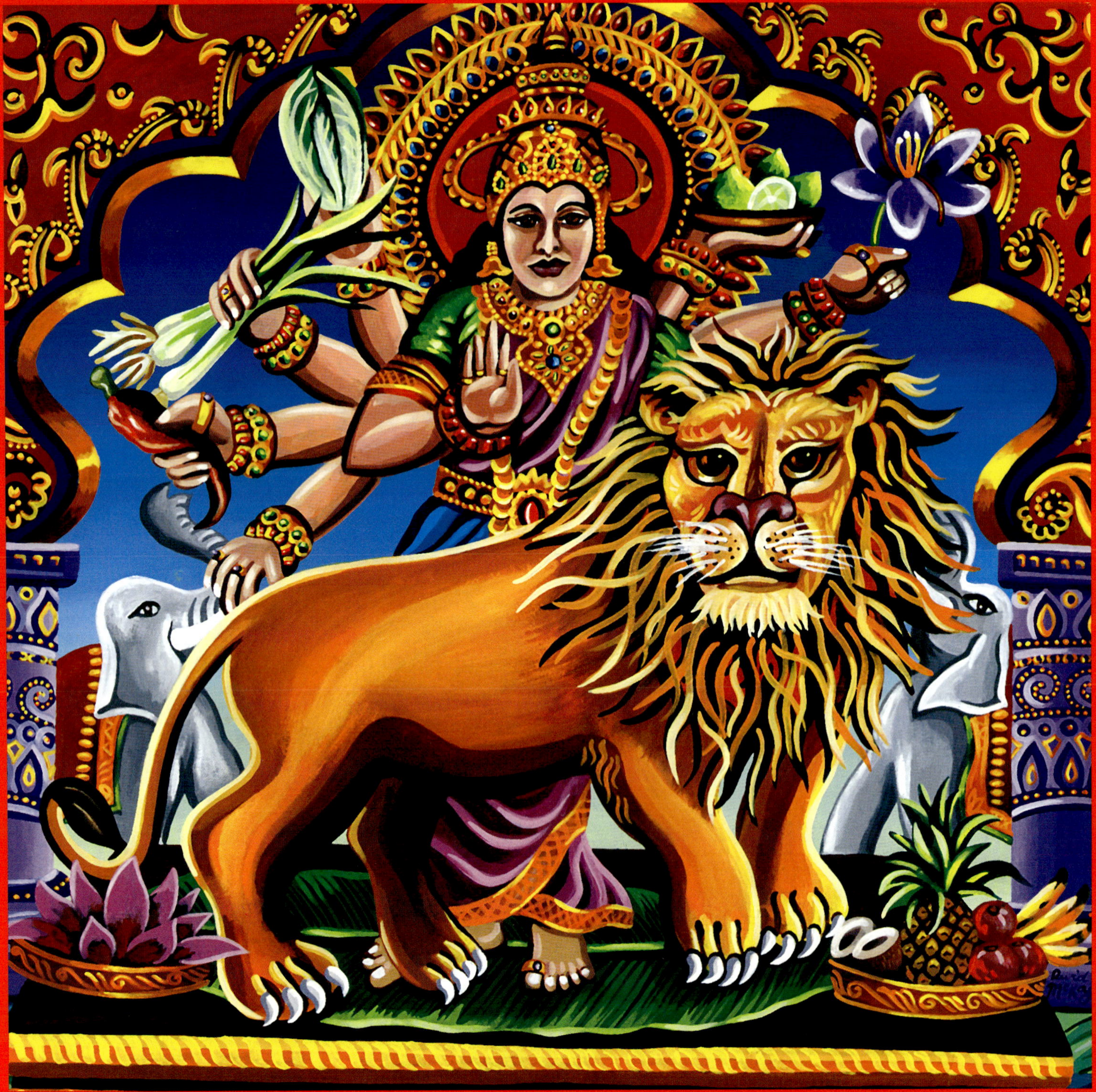

LEO
a regal indian feast

THE LEO APPETITE

The sun is the centre of the universe and so is Leo, or so they think. Glowing with a certain gilt-edged splendour this is the sign of regency and outlandish pride. Lions dine in luxury and hunt for food that is rich, aromatic and sophisticated. In their own cooking they tackle the most ambitious and complicated recipes, so obviously a Niçoise salad isn't going to impress. An Indian feast has more of the scale, spice and aura of ritual ■ This is the sign of aristocracy and delusions of aristocracy - with the Queen Mother one extreme and Madonna at the other. Ruling the heart rather than the head, the health issue for Leo is blood and circulation, so while they may lunge for rich sauces and heavy meat dishes it serves them well to dine on more elegant portions. The dishes in this Maharajah-style feast are complex but balanced. Catering to a palette that loves sweet and sour tastes, the barley and coriander cakes are accented with a cooling spiced cucumber raita, the lamb offset by sweet potato and apple curry, the savoury naan bread strewn with raisins ■ Classy little bowls of vegetable side dishes such as asparagus with black mustard seeds and cinnamon and cabbage with fennel and ginger, make the Leo feel that flavours and condiments from each corner of the earth have been gathered to trumpet their greater glory. Though it may sicken the quieter earth and water signs, these minxy kittens and growling big cats expect the red carpet to unfurl for them - from the gutter to the master bedroom of your castle. Don't just stand there you fool, pour the wine ■

It isn't always simple for the hunter to be captured by the prey. Leo is about dominance, leadership and flashes of brilliance, so somehow you must contrive to have this Sunday dinner invitation look like it was their idea. Either that or the invitation should be embossed on creamy Tiffany's paper stock and delivered by messenger. If you can't afford to have the living room sofa reupholstered in faux leopard print and the walls hung with scarlet silk velvet, at least make sure the seat reserved for Leo is stately and throne like. Others might laugh at a deckchair festooned with gold tassles and a card-board crown, but Leo would merely puff out their chest and fail to see the irony. *The key word for this rendezvous is glamour - a glowing table reflected dramatically by mirrors, cutlery set formally, brass plates [if you don't have solid gold], gilt-embossed bohemian goblets. Dandelions may be Leo's flower but broad-faced sunflowers are bolder.*

THE LEO SEDUCTION

With rich food, opulent decorations and art direction by Napoleon Bonaparte you may find the splendour that Leo demands insufferably eighties, redolent of nouveau excesses and an abuse of reflective surfaces. No doubt about it Leos are greedy [Andy Warhol, Jackie O, Shelley Winters], showy and sometimes even vulgar [Mae West, Cecil B. De Mille] but somebody in the zodiac has to be a showstopper. Razzle, dazzle, French champagne while Rome and the rest of the planet cinders to a radioactive husk. Like Coco Chanel, luxury for Leo comes before conscience - social or otherwise. This seduction is about abundance and swagger, so if you prefer your prey mousey or dreamy leave the wild cats in their den and head to the aquarium.

barley & coriander cakes with mango chutney & spiced cucumber raita **marinated lamb racks with sweet potato & apple curry** asparagus with black mustard seeds & cinnamon **cabbage with onion, fennel & ginger** raisin naan bread **roasted almond & saffron rice pilaf** spiced figs with coconut cream **indian shortbread**

a classic gimlet lassi **chilled beer** spicy sauvignon blanc drinks

barley & coriander cakes with mango chutney & spiced cucumber raita

BARLEY AND CORIANDER CAKES
1 cup barley
1 cup mashed potato
1 small onion, chopped
1 teaspoon roasted cummin seeds
1 pinch salt
1 teaspoon Garam Marsala
1 good handful coriander, chopped
2 cloves garlic, minced
1 cm piece ginger, chopped
Ghee for cooking the cakes in
Juice of 1/2 lemon
Spiced cucumber raita
1 telegraph cucumber
2 spring onions
1 clove garlic
1/2 teaspoon ground cummin
1/2 teaspoon ground coriander
1 pinch salt
Ground black pepper
1/4 teaspoon mustard seeds
2 cups plain natural yoghurt
20 fresh mint leaves

BARLEY AND CORIANDER CAKES
- Cover the barley in water and soak for at least 1 hour, rinse thoroughly and add fresh water.
- Bring barley to the boil then simmer gently until it has softened.
- Sauté off the onion, ginger and garlic.
- Add all the spices and barley to the mashed potato and combine thoroughly.
- Add the onion mix and the juice of half a lemon to the potato.
- Season to taste.
- Shape into small balls and flatten them slightly, then put them onto a plate that has been covered in cling wrap. Chill in fridge until needed.
- In a non-stick pan heat the ghee and gently fry the cakes, turning over to ensure that both sides are crisp and golden.

SPICED CUCUMBER RAITA
- Peel and slice cucumber very finely, sprinkle with the salt and leave to sit for a few minutes in a colander. Rinse and pat dry before using.
- Mix the spices with the yoghurt and add the finely chopped spring onion, garlic and fresh mint leaves.
- Add the now softened cucumber and mix well.
- Set aside in refrigerator for at least 30 minutes.
- Serve with hot barley and coriander cakes and mango chutney [store bought].

marinated lamb racks with sweet potato & apple curry

MARINATED LAMB RACKS
3 racks of lamb with 8 cutlets each [ask the butcher to trim the racks so there is some of the rib exposed]
2 cm piece ginger, grated
2 cloves garlic, minced
2 teaspoons Garam Marsala
200 ml olive oil
2 teaspoons turmeric
1 good handful fresh coriander stalks, finely chopped
Salt and pepper
1 orange and 1 lemon zest
6 curry leaves

SWEET POTATO AND APPLE CURRY
500 g sweet potato, chopped into bite-sized pieces
2 Granny Smith apples, chopped into bite-sized pieces with skin on
1 large onion, chopped finely
1 red capsicum, chopped into bite sized pieces
1 teaspoon mustard seeds
1/2 teaspoon turmeric
3 tablespoons oil or ghee
1 small piece ginger, grated
2 teaspoons mild curry paste
1 1/2 cups coconut milk
4 cloves garlic, minced
1 stick cinnamon
375 g tin tomatoes, roughly chopped

LAMB RACKS
- Mix the herbs, spices and fruit zest with the oil.
- Score the fat on the racks of lamb with a sharp knife, making sure that you don't cut into the flesh of the lamb.
- Coat the lamb generously with the spice paste and leave to marinate for at least three hours.
- Preheat the oven to 220°C.
- In a heavy bottomed pan heat 1 tablespoon of ghee, when it is hot add the racks with the skin side down. When they are well sealed turn them over and place in oven for 15 minutes [the lamb will be pink, cook further 5 minutes for medium].
- Allow the racks to rest for 10 minutes before cutting.

SWEET POTATO AND APPLE CURRY
- Heat oil or ghee in heavy based saucepan.
- Sauté the onion, garlic, ginger, mustard seeds, turmeric, curry paste and cinnamon for 5 minutes.
- Add the sweet potato and red capsicum stirring well to coat the vegetables.
- Add the chopped tomatoes and simmer until the sweet potato is tender.
- Add the apple and coconut milk and cook for 10 minutes.
- Just before serving, stir in 1 tablespoon of sweet mango chutney.

TO SERVE
- Cut racks into individual cutlets.
- Lay cutlets decoratively on a warmed serving plate beside the curry. Garnish with fresh coriander.
- Wedges of fresh lemon and orange can be served in an accompanying bowl to squeeze over the lamb.

asparagus with black mustard seeds & cinnamon

2 bunches fresh asparagus
4 tablespoons peanut oil
3 cloves garlic, minced
1 small red chilli, chopped very finely
1 teaspoon ground cinnamon
1 onion, finely sliced
2 teaspoons black mustard seeds

- Heat oil in frypan and add the mustard seeds, when they begin to pop add the garlic, onion, chilli, cinnamon and cook until the onion is browned.
- Add 20 ml of water and stir, then remove from heat.
- Bring a large pot of water to the boil with a teaspoon of salt.
- Trim the coarse ends from the asparagus and plunge into boiling water for a couple of minutes [until tender] and then quickly refresh under cold water. Set aside until ready to serve.
- To serve the asparagus, gently reheat the onion mix and add the asparagus right at the last minute to warm through.

cabbage with onion, fennel & ginger

1/2 small cabbage, preferably savoy
1 large brown onion, cut in half and sliced
3 cloves garlic, minced
2 cm piece ginger, grated finely
1/2 teaspoon ground cumin
1/2 teaspoon Garam Marsala
1/2 teaspoon fennel seeds
1 red chilli, chopped very finely
4–5 tablespoons peanut oil
Salt and pepper

- With a serrated-edged knife, shred the cabbage as finely as possible.
- Heat the oil in a non-stick pan and add the spices. Cook for a few seconds before adding the finely sliced onion.
- Sauté the onion and spices for a few minutes and then add the shredded cabbage. Continue to cook on a high heat for the first minute, then reduce the heat and continue to cook until the cabbage has wilted and been thoroughly coated with the spices.

N.B. You may find that you need to add a little extra moisture. If you have any coconut milk handy then add this, otherwise water and a touch of lemon juice will be fine.

raisin naan bread

1 1/2 cups white flour
1 1/2 cups whole-wheat flour
1 teaspoon salt
1/2 teaspoon baking powder
1/2 teaspoon sugar
120 ml warm milk
15 g fresh yeast [available at health food stores]
125 g plain yoghurt
2 tablespoons ghee
2 tablespoons raisins

- Sift the flours, salt and baking powder into a bowl.
- Dissolve the sugar into the warm milk, then stir in the broken-up yeast letting the mixture sit for 5 minutes in a warm place. Once it begins to bubble stir in the yoghurt.
- Mix this into the flour and add the raisins. Form into a soft dough and transfer onto a floured board.
- Knead the dough for about 9 minutes until it is the consistency of normal bread dough. Put the mixture back into a bowl, cover with a dry cloth and leave in a warm place to rise for 2–3 hours or until it has doubled in bulk.
- Punch the dough down and divide the mixture into 6 balls. Shape into flat ovals by slapping the dough from hand to hand until the ball lengthens and flattens. These shapes should be around 1 cm thick.
- Preheat the oven 240°C.
- Place the bread onto flat baking trays and brush the top side with ghee. Bake in the oven for approximately 7 minutes, or until the bread is golden brown.

N.B. It may seem like a lot of bother to make your own naan. However this is a very delicious recipe and has the added bonus of the seductive raisins that Leos love so much.

spiced figs with coconut cream

SPICED FIGS
12 ripe fresh figs
1 litre water
180 g brown sugar
1 vanilla pod, cut down the middle
2 cm piece ginger, peeled
2 bay leaves
4 cloves
4 pods cardamom
1 stick cinnamon
Zest of 1 lemon and 1 orange
Coconut cream
250 ml cream
1 tablespoon castor sugar
100 g shaved coconut, toasted
1 tablespoon coconut syrup [optional - available from Asian food stores]

SPICED FIGS
- Place all the ingredients except the figs into a saucepan and bring to the boil.
Once the syrup is at a rapid boil add the figs and reduce the heat to a slow simmer.
- Cook the figs for a few minutes and then remove from the hot syrup with a slotted spoon [the figs will be fragile at this stage so handle them with care] and let them cool.
- Return the syrup to the heat and reduce until it has thickened. This will take approximately 25 minutes and will enhance the flavours of the spices.
- Gently place the figs back in the syrup while it cools down keeping an eye on the figs as they shouldn't be so soft that they fall apart. If the figs are already very soft it is probably best that you wait till the syrup has cooled down before returning the figs to it.
- Serve with the chilled coconut cream and plenty of the syrup.

COCONUT CREAM
- Whip the cream with the castor sugar until it forms soft peaks [if you are using coconut syrup add this now].
- Refrigerate until just before serving. Fold in the toasted coconut and transfer to serving dish.

roasted almond & saffron rice pilaf

500 ml basmati rice, measured in a measuring cup
4 tablespoons vegetable oil or ghee
2 bay leaves
1 stick cinnamon
3 cloves garlic
5 pods cardamom
1 teaspoon salt
4 cloves
1 small onion, very finely chopped
1/4 cup sultanas
1/2 cup roasted almonds
1 teaspoon ground turmeric
1/2 teaspoon saffron powder
1 handful fresh coriander, chopped
750 ml chicken stock or water

- Wash the rice under cold running water for a couple of minutes to remove the starch, then drain in a colander over a bowl.
- Put the oil or ghee into a heavy bottomed saucepan and set over a medium heat. When the oil is hot add the onion, cloves, garlic, bay leaves, cardamom, cinnamon and salt. Stir thoroughly and cook till the onions have softened slightly.
- Add the turmeric, saffron and rice and stir well to coat the rice. Cook the rice for a few minutes stirring gently.
- Now add the stock or water and bring to the boil. Once it is boiling reduce the heat to very low, cover the saucepan with a tight lid and cook for 20–25 minutes.
- Once rice is cooked turn it out into a serving bowl and sprinkle generously with the roasted almonds, sultanas and chopped coriander.

indian shortbread

125 g ghee
1/2 cup castor sugar
1 cup fine semolina
1/4 cup plain flour
1 teaspoon ground cardamom
1 teaspoon fennel seeds

- Cream the ghee and sugar together until light and fluffy.
- Add the sieved semolina, flour, cardamom and fennel seeds and mix well. Allow the mix to rest for 30 minutes.
- Take a tablespoon of the mixture and roll into a ball and flatten slightly.
- Place onto a greased baking tray leaving some space between the biscuits so they can spread.
- Preheat oven to 160°C and bake until golden brown.

classic gimlet

1 jigger dry gin
1/2 teaspoon lime cordial
1/2 teaspoon sugar syrup [optional]
1 slice fresh lime

- Take a wide-mouthed champagne glass and put in the gin, followed by the lime cordial.
- Stir in the sugar syrup [this may be needed to take away the bitterness of the lime cordial].
- Fill the rest of the glass with chilled water adding an ice cube and a slice of lime.

lassi

150 ml yoghurt
1 tablespoon castor sugar
200 ml iced water
Fruit of choice or mint leaves and rosewater
Ice cubes

- Blend all ingredients in a blender until frothy.

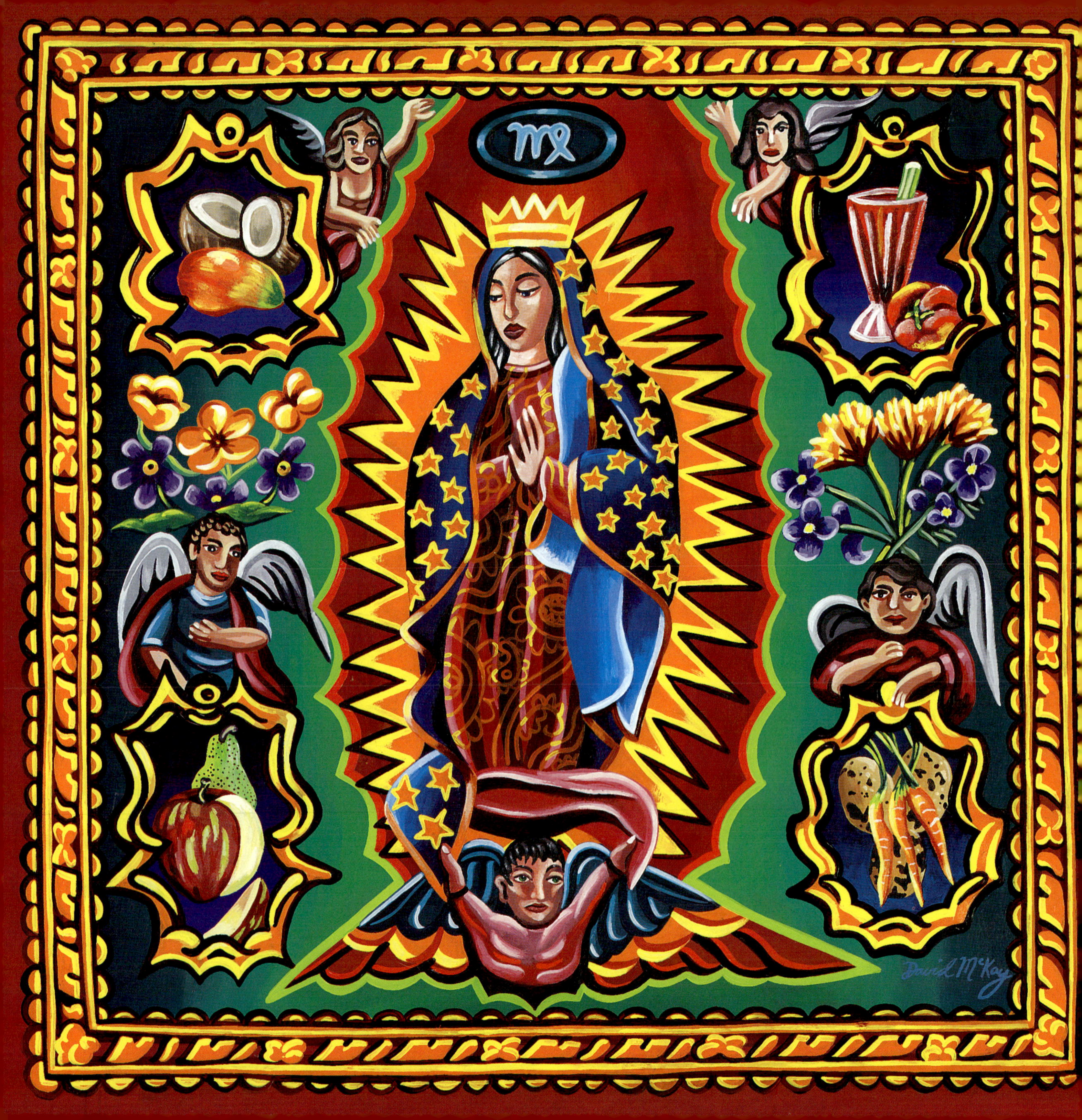
David McKay

VIRGO
sunday brunch

THE VIRGO APPETITE

What are the associations that immediately spring to mind when you hear the word 'virgin'? Be honest. Pure, untouched, prissy … uptight? Neat, tidy Virgos suffer from precisely this sort of image crisis. They are the fuss budgets and Swiss clocks of the zodiac, the alphabetical order purists that make life a living hell for sloppy, intuitive water signs and passionate, impatient fire signs. Virgos make you anxious about kitchen cleanliness, at their worst they check the use-by dates on your ingredients when your back is turned and make sure the olive oil is cold pressed extra extra virgin Nutritionally sensitive and focused on perfection, they can tell you the caloric and mineral content of the dishes you timidly dare to serve them and make a high-pitched noise like an oven timer way before the garlic bread starts burning. Critical and highly strung, the virgin appetite leans towards the herbal, favouring the subtle green flavours of endive, chicory, fennel and dill Like Gemini they are governed by Mercury, so game birds and nutty flavours [coconut, hazelnut] are also on the menu, balanced by the perfectly wholesome flavours of oats and rye. The best term to define Virgo tastebuds is - alert. This is food that's sensible rather than sensual, attending to the needs of the mind and the body with a precise tabular content of vitamins, fibre and essential fatty acids. The perfect Virgo brunch leaves no culinary stone unturned - wholesome muesli, comforting baked beans, savoury duck liver and pesto morsels justified by the earthy base of a whole-wheat pancake will meet their stringent dictums. For dessert you may be reckless and serve the slightly naughty coconut and almond syrup cake as long as it is balanced by fresh mango. Some Virgos sneak candy bars into their diets but these are rare fugitives from the flock, think again of the virgin - beacon of the pure and quite sensitive to garlic.

THE VIRGO SEDUCTION

Hate to say it but many Virgos are morning people. Vile types who pound their chest at dawn and proclaim 'Carpe Diem, baby!' as they skull a shooter of wheat grass juice and then go lunging at tax audits and other unpleasant tasks with undisguised glee. How do you lure one of these organisational Amazons into a state of erotic abandon? Play it their way. Scrub your dark fantasies down with with lemon juice and smuggle your hidden desires into the starched envelope of early daylight. After something sprightly like tennis or jogging whisk your sweet thing into a room whiter than a dental laboratory. White china, white linen, white lilies of the valley, hey, go crazy and drink half a litre of milk straight from the carton right in front of them. But don't lose your grip on the big picture for a second. Nothing about this brunch is vague or messy. Each gorgeous healthy course arrives at the table in ordered sequence, and your eyes remain shiny, patient and calm as they check your silverware for smudge prints. The conversation is focused on health issues [patiently tolerate tales of their extensive medical history], science, career moves and the humour of Stuart Littlemore [fusspot fact-checker from hell]. If you disappear to floss in between courses they won't object, if you offer vitamins as a chaser to the Bloody Mary, all the better • When it comes to compliments, present a typed list with a cross catalogue of the time and dates on which these warm visions entered your mind. Delay is central to a great seduction but it is very hard to delay a Virgo. When they start to anxiously gaze at their watch ask them to help you search for your Filofax [somewhere under the bed] or suggest a shower for some good, clean soapy fun. Ceres, the goddess of control, would concede to such ordered pleasures. But be quick! Your allotted time starts now •

fresh apple & pear muesli baked beans with roasted tomato & basil **grilled duck livers served with parsley & hazelnut pesto on whole-wheat pancakes** mushroom caps filled with chicken & marjoram **toasted rye bread with smoked salmon & a fennel & cucumber salad with dill mayonnaise** coconut & almond syrup cake with fresh mango salad

lime & peach wine spritzers bloody mary

drinks

fresh apple & pear muesli

2 cups rolled oats
2 cups milk
1/2 cup natural yoghurt
2 tablespoons chopped hazelnuts and almonds
1 Granny Smith apple, grated
1 large pear, grated
2 tablespoons honey
1 punnet strawberries or raspberries

- Soak the oats overnight in the milk.
- The next morning mix in the honey, nuts, grated apple and pear.
- Serve with fresh berries and yoghurt.

baked beans with roasted tomato & basil

375 g haricot beans, soaked overnight
1 large brown onion, finely chopped
1 red capsicum, diced
2 sticks celery, finely chopped
2 tablespoons maple syrup
400 g tin peeled tomatoes, puréed
12 Roma tomatoes
2 bay leaves
2 sprigs thyme
2 cloves garlic, minced
1 bunch fresh basil
Salt and pepper
Tabasco sauce [optional]
2 bacon rinds
3 tablespoons olive oil

MIREPOIX
1 stick celery
1 onion
4 cloves garlic, chopped into slices
1 sprig thyme
1 bay leaf

- Rinse the soaked beans and put into saucepan with chopped vegetable mirepoix. Cover with water and bring to the boil.
- Cook the beans until just tender, strain [reserving the cooking liquid] and refresh beans under cold water - discard the mirepoix.
- Heat oil in a heavy bottomed saucepan and sauté the onion, garlic, celery and bacon rinds, cooking until the onion is soft.
- Add the red capsicum, bay leaves and thyme, cook for a further minute before adding the beans and tomato purée
- Pour in reserved bean liquid until the beans are covered and cook over a gentle heat for approximately 11/2 hours. The sauce should be slightly thick and rich and the beans soft.
- Add the maple syrup and season well with salt, pepper and tabasco sauce.
- While the beans are cooking cut the Romas in half lengthways and season with salt and pepper.
- Drizzle generously with olive oil and place in 180°C oven to roast until slightly caramelised and well roasted [approximately 30–40 minutes].
- Serve the beans with the roasted tomatoes adding freshly chopped basil right at the last minute.

N.B Tinned baked beans are no substitute for this home-made variety.

grilled duck livers served with parsley & hazelnut pesto on whole-wheat pancakes

GRILLED DUCK LIVERS

250 g duck or chicken livers, cleaned
2 tablespoons olive oil
1 tablespoon balsamic vinegar
1 tablespoon butter
Salt and pepper

WHOLE WHEAT PANCAKES

235 g whole-wheat flour
1 tablespoon active dry yeast
1 teaspoon sugar
1 egg
300 ml milk
60 ml warm water
1/4 teaspoon Salt

PARSLEY AND HAZELNUT PESTO

1 cup each fresh continental parsley & basil leaves
2 cloves garlic
1/2 cup oil
3 tablespoons roasted hazelnuts
2 tablespoons freshly grated parmesan
1/4 lemon rind
Salt to taste

GRILLED DUCK LIVERS
- Heat half the oil in a heavy bottomed pan.
- When oil is very hot, place half the livers very carefully.
- Seal the livers very quickly remove and rest.
- Repeat with remaining livers.
- When all the livers are cooked, pour in the balsamic vinegar and the butter. Season with salt and pepper.
- When the butter is melted add the livers and coat with the glossy sauce.

WHOLE-WHEAT PANCAKES
- Combine the yeast, sugar and warm water - set aside until foamy [approximately 10 minutes].
- Sift the flour and salt together in a bowl making a well in the centre of the flour and add the yeast mixture.
- In a small bowl beat together the egg and milk.
- Stir into the flour gradually and mix until a smooth batter is formed. Cover the bowl and let sit for 1 hour.

TO COOK
- Brush the bottom of a heavy based frypan with oil.
- Drop tablespoons of batter onto the pan and cook until small bubbles appear.
- Turn the pancakes and cook until golden brown.
N.B. The pancakes can be kept warm in a low oven.

PARSLEY AND HAZELNUT PESTO
- In a food processor combine all ingredients except the oil and form a fine paste.
- With the motor still running add the oil in a steady stream.

TO SERVE
- Arrange warm pancakes on a platter.
- Place a generous amount of pesto onto each pancake then finish with a glazed duck liver.

mushroom caps filled with chicken & marjoram

12 large capped mushrooms
2 tablespoons olive oil
1 onion, chopped
2 cloves garlic, chopped
2 sprigs fresh marjoram
1/4 teaspoon nutmeg
1 teaspoon lemon zest
150 g minced chicken
1 tablespoon ground walnuts
150 ml white wine
Salt and pepper

- Remove the stems from the mushrooms and chop them finely, reserve the caps.
- Heat the olive oil in a frypan and sauté the garlic and onion for about 5 minutes.
- Add the chicken mince and mushroom stalks and cook for a further 5 minutes.
- Mix in the nutmeg, lemon zest, marjoram and walnut meal. Season with salt and pepper and set to one side.
- Place mushroom caps in a baking pan and fill with the chicken mix.
- Drizzle with olive oil and some white wine, cover with foil and cook in 180°C oven for about 15 minutes.
- Remove foil and continue cooking for another 5 minutes.
- Serve warm with chopped marjoram sprinkled generously over the top.

toasted rye bread with smoked salmon & a fennel & cucumber salad with dill mayonnaise

1 loaf light rye bread
12 thin slices smoked salmon
1 small bulb fennel
1 telegraph cucumber
1/4 bunch fresh dill
Salt and pepper
2 tablespoons mayonnaise [preferably home-made]
Juice of 1/2 lemon

- Peel the cucumber and slice down the middle lengthways removing the seeds with a teaspoon.
- Slice cucumber as finely as possible, place it in a colander and sprinkle liberally with salt - allow to drain for at least half an hour.
- Trim the outside skin and the hard stalks from the fennel and cut in half lengthways.
- Wash the inside part of the fennel very thoroughly and slice it as finely as possible. Place it into a bowl of water with the lemon juice in it.
- Rinse the cucumber very well under cold water and pat dry with a paper towel.
- Remove the fennel from the water and pat dry
- Mix the two together in a bowl and add the chopped dill and the mayonnaise. Add the seasoning and mix well.

TO SERVE
- Slice the rye bread into 6 thinnish slices and toast - keep the toast warm in the oven while cooking the rest.
- Cut the toast in half, spoon a bit of the cucumber and fennel salad onto each piece and finish with a swirl of smoked salmon, cracked black pepper and a sprig of dill.
- Wedges of lemon on the side of the plate are optional.

coconut & almond syrup cake with fresh mango salad

125 g butter
1 cup castor sugar
4 eggs
1 1/2 cups desiccated coconut
1/2 cup almond meal
1 cup self-raising flour

LEMON SYRUP
1 cup sugar
2/3 cup water
Zest of 1 lemon

FRESH MANGO SALAD
2 perfectly ripe mangoes
1 punnet strawberries or raspberries
Juice of 1 lime
150 ml whipped cream
Toasted coconut flakes for garnish

COCONUT AND ALMOND SYRUP CAKE
• Butter and flour a 20 cm ring tin.
• Cream the butter and sugar in a bowl with an electric mixer until light and fluffy. Then add the eggs one at a time beating continuously until the mixture is combined.
• Fold in the coconut, almond meal and the sifted flour by hand.
• Pour mix into cake tin and bake in a 180°C [moderately slow] oven for about 45 minutes.
• When cooked remove from oven and pour over the syrup immediately. Allow to cool in pan. Serve with fresh mango salad.

LEMON SYRUP
• Combine all the ingredients in a saucepan and stir over heat until the sugar has dissolved.
• Bring to the boil and then simmer for 5 minutes.
• Strain the syrup before pouring over the cake.

FRESH MANGO SALAD
• Slice the mango from the seed and place in a bowl with the lime juice - set aside for half an hour before adding the berries.
• Serve chilled with the coconut and almond syrup cake, some freshly whipped cream and toasted coconut flakes.

DRINKS

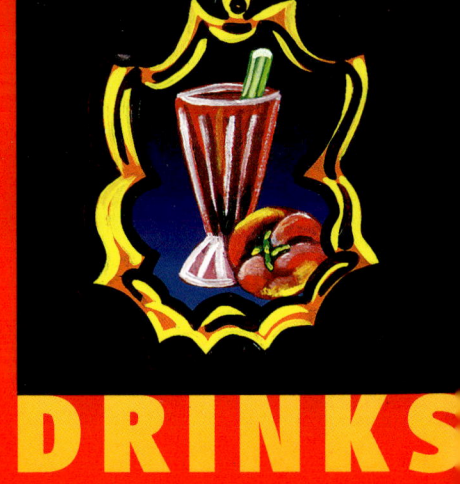

lime & peach wine spritzers

1 bottle white wine
1 bottle sparkling mineral water
Juice of 3 limes
2 ripe peaches, skinned and puréed
Mint leaves for garnish
6 lumps of sugar

- Combine all the ingredients [except the mint leaves].
- Place 1 lump of sugar into the bottom of the glass and pour over the wine spritzer. Garnish with a fresh mint leaf.

bloody mary

300 ml vodka
3 cups tomato juice
Juice of 1 lime
2 teaspoons Worcestershire sauce
Freshly ground black pepper to taste
2 teaspoons horseradish
Garnish
1 Lebanese cucumber
1 stick celery
2 spring onions
1/2 red capsicum
1 tomato
8 leaves basil
Sea salt to taste

- Chop all the garnish vegetables into a fine dice and mix with the freshly chopped basil leaves.
- Mix the vodka, tomato juice, lime juice, Worcestershire sauce, horseradish and pepper together in a glass jug.
- Pour into long glasses of ice and garnish with the vegetable mix and a sprinkle of sea salt.

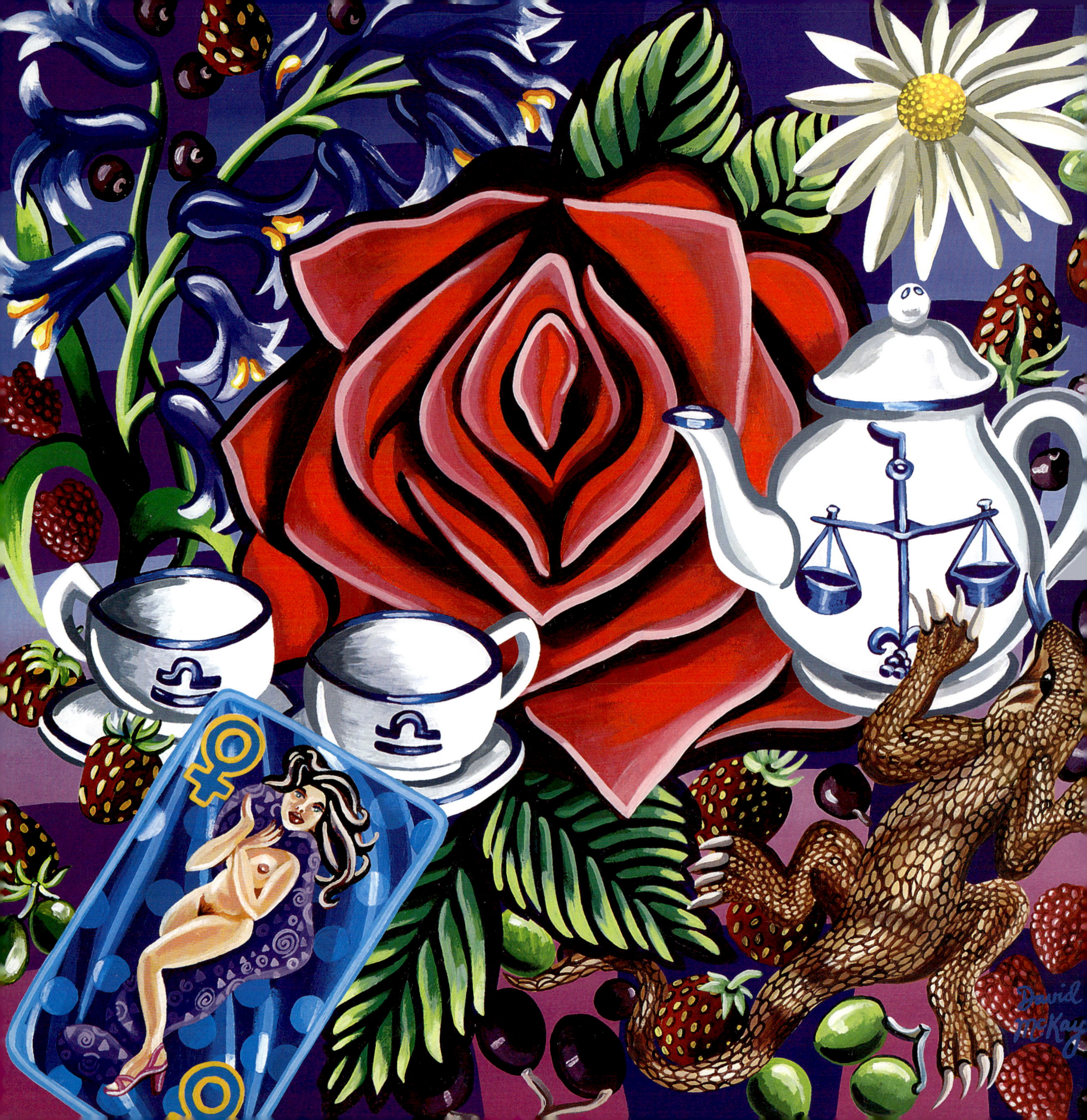
David

Libra
afternoonteaparty

THE LIBRA APPETITE

Imagine living in a world where every man is a fop and every woman a beauty queen. A glittering ballroom, where billowing silk curtains in tall French doorways dust the floor scattered with fallen rosebuds and slow serenades haunt the air. Sound like a Bryan Ferry video to you? Welcome to Libraland. Oh yes, its all very tasteful for these lounge lizards. Libra takes this Venus goddess of love thing quite literally. They live life like the Impulse commercials of old, springing from nowhere bearing bouquets of violets and full-blown roses or expecting wheel barrows of daisies to block their path. Chill the glasses, iron the damask and obscure that stubbie from sight, this is an appetite driven by aesthetics rather than raw sensuality. Unlike the bovine Taurus [also ruled by Venus], Librans are charmed by the piquant rather than the meaty. The non-citrus sweet fruits of summer and the perfumed herbs of the high minded - mint and sorrel - delight them. Divine little cakey things, finger sandwiches and sweet morsels made of figs and peaches tickle their rather saccharine tastebuds. Although famously sugary, this is also the sign of the scales. To demonstrate refinement, a balance must be struck between the gooey desert wine they love and the tangy watercress they need, and rich shortbreads should be served with tea taken black. While other more lusty beings might sniff at such a teddy bear's picnic, Librans find pretty things sexy. Dining lightly in the afternoon befits a love god or goddess for the mood is indolent and the decadence veiled by wholesome dappled sunlight.

In the the twenties they perfected the tea dance. A prim affair where boys in pale flannel suits pressed their enthusiasms against the legs of girls in gauzy dresses, quaffing sugar-dusted pastries in between. As these halls of pastel-tinted lust no longer exist you must flick your dancecard towards your chosen son/daughter of Venus and ask them instead to tea 'at home' or perhaps set up in a disused Victorian gazebo. To get this right you'll have to indulge your sympathies for fusspots. Remember, the mother of 'proper' etiquette herself, Emily Post, was a Libran. Sensitive, brainy Montgomery Clift was also a Libran. These people have class! Select your colours from scrupulously researching the Chinese ceramic section of the nearest State gallery and conjure the most delicate equation of pink, pale green and aqua blue that you can find. Details! The tea cups themselves must be fine and light, like the skin of a pearl, the pot mustn't dribble and the bouquet must breathe with the lush opulence of a still life by Manet -

THE LIBRA SEDUCTION

hydrangeas, violets, bluebells, dusty Julia and velvet petalled Lincoln roses • The intimacy of tea for two won't deter a Libran, indeed they prefer a perfect partnership to a sloppy sprawl of kids, dogs and aquaintances across the picnic blanket. Wherever you are with the Libran try to evoke the spirit of the great salons of Europe, the turf of dandies and professional beauties. Converse about art for art's sake, the aesthetics of Islamic architecture, the amusing difference between being nude and being naked [detail!] then move onto topics like the criminal justice system. The key to this seduction is symmetry - a balance must be struck between froth and intensity, decoration and substance, charm and integrity, pleasure and politics and, most importantly, sugar and spice •

finger sandwiches [chicken & watercress, cucumber celery & almond & cream cheese] balmoral biscuits **glazed peach tartlets** fig shortbreads **warm scones served with raspberry & blackberry compote & mascarpone** pimms with cucumber, orange, strawberries & borage
drinks peppermint tea **earl grey tea**

finger sandwiches

Bread of your choice - white, brown, whole grain
Softened butter for spreading

CHICKEN AND WATERCRESS SANDWICHES
1 small bunch watercress
1 breast of chicken, cooked
2 tablespoons good quality mayonnaise
Salt and pepper
1 bunch chopped chives

- Pick over the watercress very carefully, removing any yellow bits and all large stalks. Wash well and dry.
- Chop the chicken breast meat very finely. Combine in a bowl the chicken, mayonnaise, chopped chives, salt and pepper. Mix thoroughly.
- Make up the sandwiches and remove the crusts.
- Cut into fingers and keep very well covered until needed.

CUCUMBER SANDWICHES
1 telegraph cucumber, peeled, cut in half and seeded
Salt and pepper
Smoked salmon [optional]

- Cut the cucumber as finely as possible. Put it into a colander and sprinkle with salt. leave to stand 15 minutes.
- Rinse of all the salt and pat dry.
- If using smoked salmon, layer across the cucumber.
- Make up the sandwiches, trim off the crusts and cut into fingers.
- Keep very well covered till needed.

CELERY, ALMOND & CREAM CHEESE SANDWICHES
2 sticks celery
30 g roasted almond slivers
2 tablespoons cream cheese
Salt and pepper

- Chop the celery very finely.
- Combine all ingredients in a bowl, mix through thoroughly.
- Make up the sandwiches. Cut off the crusts and cover very well until needed.

balmoral biscuits

500 g chopped dates
21/2 cups plain flour, sifted
4 handfuls mixed peel
3/4 cup desiccated coconut
2 cups sultanas
2 heaped teaspoons bicarb soda
170 g melted butter
1 cup white sugar
1/2 cup brown sugar
1 whole egg
1 teaspoon vanilla
2 tablespoons hot water

- Preheat oven to 180°C.
- Mix all the dry ingredients together.
- Dissolve the bicarb in the hot water and add the melted butter to it.
- Add the two types of sugar.
- Add the beaten egg and vanilla. Mix together well.
- Shape into balls and flatten with a spoon. Bake for approximately 15 minutes or until golden brown.

glazed peach tartlets

3 sheets puff pastry
2–3 peaches - slipstones preferably
1 cup water
1 cup sugar
Zest of 1 orange
1 stick cinnamon

GLAZE
1 tablespoon apricot jam
1 tablespoon syrup [from the poaching]

- Using a pastry cutter, cut out 12 pastry rings from the puff pastry. Lay them flat on a baking tray and place in the fridge for 1/2 hour while you preheat the oven to 220°C and poach the peaches.
- Cut a criss-cross in the base of each peach.
- Bring the sugar, water, cinnamon and orange zest to the boil. Once boiling, drop the peaches and cook till they are just tender.
- Remove from the syrup and peel off the skin. Cut the peaches in half and slice each cheek finely.
- Take the pastry from the refrigerator and brush each round with egg white wash and gently lay the peach around each ring to make a pretty fan shape.
- Bake in the oven for 12–15 minutes until the pastry is puffed and golden.
- Bring the apricot jam and syrup to the boil - let cool slightly.
- While still hot from the oven, brush the peaches with the apricot glaze.
- Dust with icing sugar and serve hot or cold.

fig shortbreads

SHORTBREAD
90 g icing sugar
185 g plain flour
250 g butter, cut into small pieces
60 g cornflour
30 g almond meal
Vanilla essence

FIG COMPOTE
150 g dried figs chopped
Zest of 1 orange
2 tablespoons brown sugar
100 ml water

SHORTBREADS
- Preheat oven to 180°C.
- Sift together the icing sugar, flour and cornflour into a bowl. Add the almond meal and vanilla. With your fingers, rub in the butter until there are no obvious lumps. Turn onto a lightly floured board and knead with your hands quickly to form a smooth dough.
- Place paper patty tins onto a flat baking tray. Spoon the dough into the tins and with the flat side of a spoon, flatten the top slightly.
- Bake the shortbread for about 10–15 minutes. Remove from the oven and with the handle end of a wooden spoon make an indentation into the middle of the biscuit. This will be filled with the fig compote.
- Allow to cool before removing the paper case.
- Before serving, place the shortbread onto a cake platter, dust generously with icing sugar and then fill the cases with the fig compote.

FIG COMPOTE
- Cut the figs up into small pieces and place in a saucepan with the orange zest.
- Pour over a couple of tablespoons of water and brown sugar. Bring to the boil and remove from the heat at once.
- Let the figs cool down and with a fork mash them up so that they form a jam-like consistency.

warm scones served with raspberry & blackberry compote & mascarpone

SCONES
250 g plain flour
2 teaspoons baking soda
250 ml cream
2 teaspoons sugar
Zest of 1 lemon
Zest of 1 orange
80 g butter, cut into small pieces
1 teaspoon salt

RASPBERRY AND BLACKBERRY COMPOTE
1 punnet raspberries
1 punnet blackberries
100 g sugar
Sprinkling of cinnamon
Juice of 1 orange
50 ml water
Serve with
1 packet mascarpone

- Preheat oven to 220°C.
- Combine the flour, baking powder, salt and sugar in a bowl. Add the butter, and using either a pastry cutter or your fingers, combine with the flour very quickly. Mixture should resemble breadcrumbs.
- Make a well in the centre and add the cream and fruit zest. Quickly combine into the flour mixture, kneading the dough to form a smooth non-sticky ball.
- Pat the dough to make a 1 cm thick square. Cut out 12 rounds and place on a flat baking tray. Brush the tops with milk and bake for 12–15 minutes.
- These are best eaten straight from the oven with large dollops of mascarpone and the berry compote. However, they can be made in advance and reheated.

Raspberry and blackberry compote
- Combine the sugar, orange juice, water and cinnamon in a small saucepan and bring to the boil.
- Add the berries, stir gently and turn off the heat.

pimms with cucumber, orange, strawberries & borage

Pimms No.1 Cup
Lemonade
Ginger beer
Cucumber, cut into fine strips
Orange, sliced in half moons
Strawberries, halved
Borage leaves

• Mix together all the liquids in jug[s], garnish with cucumber, borage and strawberries and orange.
• Serve in tall glasses over ice.

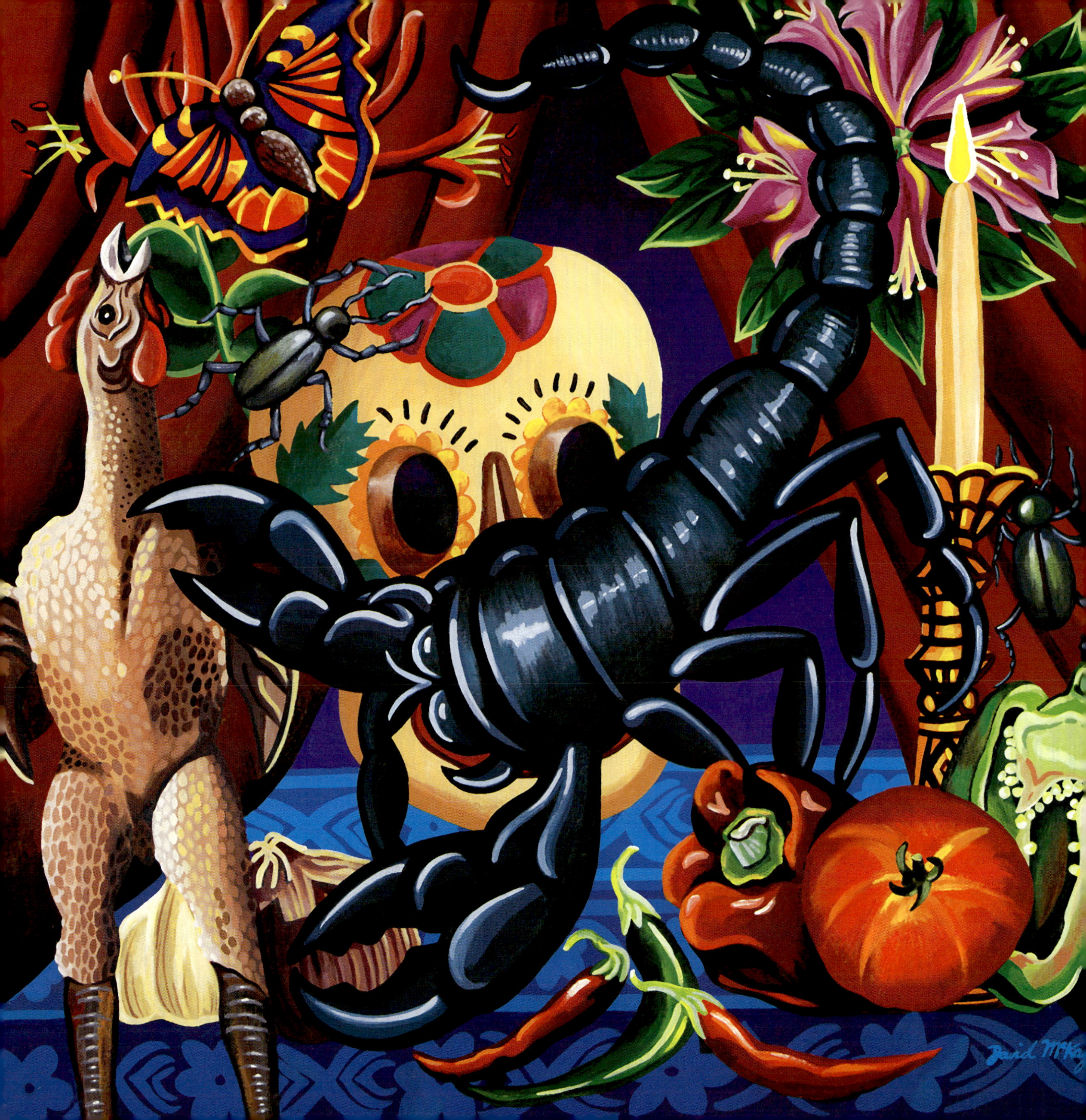

scorpio PABLO'S PASSION

THE SCORPIO APPETITE

Some like it heavy, some like it spicy and some like it hot. Scorpio likes it like all of that. It is flamenco; a swirling flame of red and black with a sting in its tail. It is Opera; gruesome and dramatic. It is dry, pungent, spicy, bitter flavours, blood-red vegetables and fruits and tamarind, cayenne and ginger. It's stimulants baby, with a capital Ssss and throw in some chilli while you're at it. Don't get dainty or wholesome and ask a Scorpio to smoke outside, don't worry about PC nutrition, leave the careful slicing of ingredients to Taurus and the retentive tidiness to Virgo. Instead, cook for Scorpio like you'd cook for Picasso in his seventies. Like it's a matter of love and death • Ruled by Pluto, god of the underworld, the mythology of Scorpio concerns dark pleasures. Steaming black coffee, blood-red wine, bull fights, black lace, Nick Cave, and Venus in furs • Why so Gothic? Why so kinky? Scorpio resides traditionally in the night of winter, the months chosen for ancient rituals that link the living with the dead. Halloween, held on 31 October, and the fantastic Latin American tradition of Dias de los Muertos [Day of the Dead] held on 1 and 2 November are the cheerful little get togethers of Scorpio. Obviously these children of the night crave food soaked in ritual, so you must approach this feast with silent film star drama • Crescendo one: arrange those squid with a serpentine coil and stuff their dark hearts with inky black rice. Passionate outburst two: build your 'Pablo Picasso' chicken casserole on a bedrock of [almost] fermented herbs and spicy tomato pastes deeper than Hades. Smouldering prelude three: cool the burning lake of desire with a chilled Rioja and lush prune and vanilla nougat. Glare if you have to, then sit down so your legs don't shake •

THE SCORPIO SEDUCTION

Don't just feed, compell! To seduce a Scorpio forget Ikea and think Bela Lugosi. Seal off the immediate area from sunlight, small blond scatter children, and anything scrubbed or touched by the hand of Country Road. Design a room that feels like a chamber and fear not the velvet. For decor consultancy refer to Keith Richards at the height of his debauched rock aristocracy [Beggars Banquet] or better still picture Bram Stoker at home. Would the father of Vlad the Impaler sit around eating seared tuna in a stainless-steel kitchen listening to Crowded House? I don't think so. Scorpion man wants it painted black, Scorpio woman wants her penetrating gaze bathed in the ambiguous flickering of candlelight. The heady scent of honeysuckle is nestled in thorns. Perfect. The table ornaments - a wrought candelabra, goblets instead of glasses, a midnight-blue cloth that bleeds into the shadows and scarlet napkins dark enough to absorb lipstick or blood or whatever. Pleasing. A palette pricked by garlic and teased with tart red currants. Better. The air is pierced with gypsy drums, a Catalan love ballad, a Cuban conga or a demure Operatic saga like Bluebeard's Castle. All of this and then many unbroken, soul-pulverising stares will do nicely. But be careful! Try not to leave the kitchen light on or let a radio alarm suddenly come bleeping through the haze of your passion pit. This is not a jaffle and a chat, it's an encounter, an unholy mass, a tryst and the last supper. Do you think you can hack the morbid pace and sustain the inky depths? Any feeble attempt at Scorpio seduction has the makings of a fiasco, turning your living room into an Addams Family salon and your kitchen into the cabinet of Dr Caligari. Spooky stuff.

squid stuffed with black rice **chilled tomato & red capsicum soup with fresh prawns** pablo's chicken with potatoes & aioli **prune & vanilla nougat served with coconut crunchies**

drinks ice-cold beer with the squid rioja with pablo's chicken **a sweet botrytis-affected riesling**

squid stuffed with black rice

6 baby squid, cleaned
Reserved squid ink
150 g arborio rice
1 onion
2 cloves garlic
60 ml white wine
500 ml fish stock
5 leaves basil
2 tablespoons olive oil
20 g butter

- Heat the fish stock
- To clean the squid, remove the ink sack and collect the ink by squeezing the sack with your fingers into a bowl, the cellophane back bone, and tentacles. Wash out the tube thoroughly and pat dry.
- Melt the butter and the olive oil together. Add the onion and garlic to sauté for a couple of minutes before adding the rice. When the rice is transparent, pour in the white wine and cook till it has been absorbed by the rice.
- Add a ladle of the fish stock and continue to stir until this has also been absorbed. Continue this process until the rice is cooked and then add the squid ink and chopped basil leaves.
- When the risotto has cooled, spoon it into the squid tubes very carefully, ensuring that you don't split the tubes. Close the end of the tube and seal with a toothpick.
- Sauté the squids in olive oil over a low heat until they have coloured slightly all over.
- Cut into slices and serve warm on garlic croûtes.

chilled red capsicum & tomato soup with fresh prawns

2 red capsicums
1 1/2 kg ripe tomatoes
1 telegraph cucumber, peeled
3 celery sticks
3 cloves garlic
1 onion
3 tablespoons extra virgin olive oil
1 tablespoon balsamic vinegar
Basil leaves
Salt and pepper
Garnish
Red capsicum
Shallot
Croûtes
Cucumber
12 prawns, cooked and peeled

- Wash capsicums, tomatoes and other vegetables thoroughly, chop into chunks. Having peeled cucumber, save 1/4 for garnish.
- Place tomatoes, cucumber, celery, garlic, onion and basil in food processor - this may involve several loads. Purée and pass though fine sieve, discard pulp. Add oil, vinegar, salt and pepper.
- Dice capsicum, shallot and cucumber for garnish.
- Just before serving, give soup a good stir as it will have separated. Ladle into soup bowls and garnish with chopped vegetables and prawns.

pablo's chicken with potatoes & aioli

CHICKEN
1 chicken, cut into pieces
2 onions
12 cloves garlic, unpeeled
12 chat potatoes, cut in half
250 ml dry white wine
100 ml sherry
50 ml olive oil
2 sprigs thyme
2 sprigs rosemary
8 sage leaves
2 bay leaves
2 teaspoons paprika
2 small red chillis, seeded and chopped finely
75 g pine nuts, toasted
150 ml chicken stock
1/2 bunch chopped parsley
Salt and pepper

AIOLI
5 cloves garlic
2 egg yolks
1 tablespoon Dijon mustard
2 tablespoons white wine vinegar
250 ml olive oil

CHICKEN
- Preheat the oven to 210°C.
- Peel and slice the onions. In a heavy bottomed, oven-proof casserole dish, sauté the onions and garlic with the thyme, rosemary and paprika in the olive oil.
- Add the chicken and brown on all sides.
- Add the wine, sherry, stock, potatoes, sage leaves, bay leaves and chilli. Cover with a lid and place in the oven for 25–30 minutes.
- Finish with the toasted pine nuts and chopped parsley. Serve with aioli and crusty french bread.

AIOLI
- Roast garlic cloves in their skin. Remove and mash. Place garlic, egg yolks, vinegar, mustard and salt in a food processor. Blend the ingredients and slowly add the olive oil in a slow stream.

prune & vanilla nougat served with coconut crunchies

NOUGAT
125 g prunes, pitted
500 g sugar
2 drops vanilla essence
1 stick cinnamon
1/2 teaspoon cream of tartar
2 tablespoons brandy
375 ml water
6 egg whites

COCONUT CRUNCHIES
250 ml finely shredded coconut
250 ml granulated sugar
250 ml unsalted butter, cut into small pieces
500 ml flour
1 egg
1 teaspoon lemon juice
1 teaspoon baking powder
1/4 teaspoon salt

NOUGAT
- Purée the prunes in a blender with the water. Add the sugar, vanilla and cinnamon and purée again.
- Cook the purée over a medium heat to 110°C on a sugar thermometer.
- In a large bowl, beat the egg whites into a froth. Add the cream of tartar and beat further until it forms stiff peaks. Add the prune purée in a slow stream and beat further until the mixture cools. Finally, stir in the brandy.
- The nougat can be served either chilled, in individual bowls, or frozen, like ice cream, with coconut crunchies.

COCONUT CRUNCHIES
- Briefly process the sugar in a food processor with a steel blade.
- Add the coconut and blend further whilst gradually adding the butter. Blend until creamy. Add the egg and lemon juice and briefly combine. Now add the flour, baking powder and salt and blend, again briefly, into a dough.
- Refrigerate the dough for 15 minutes.
- Preheat oven to 200°C.
- Roll out the dough to thickness of approximately 1/2 cm and cut out biscuit shapes measuring roughly 6 cm in diameter. Placing these on greaseproof paper, brush lightly with water and dust lightly with a little additional coconut.
- Bake for 9–10 minutes when the edges will have browned. Remove and cool.

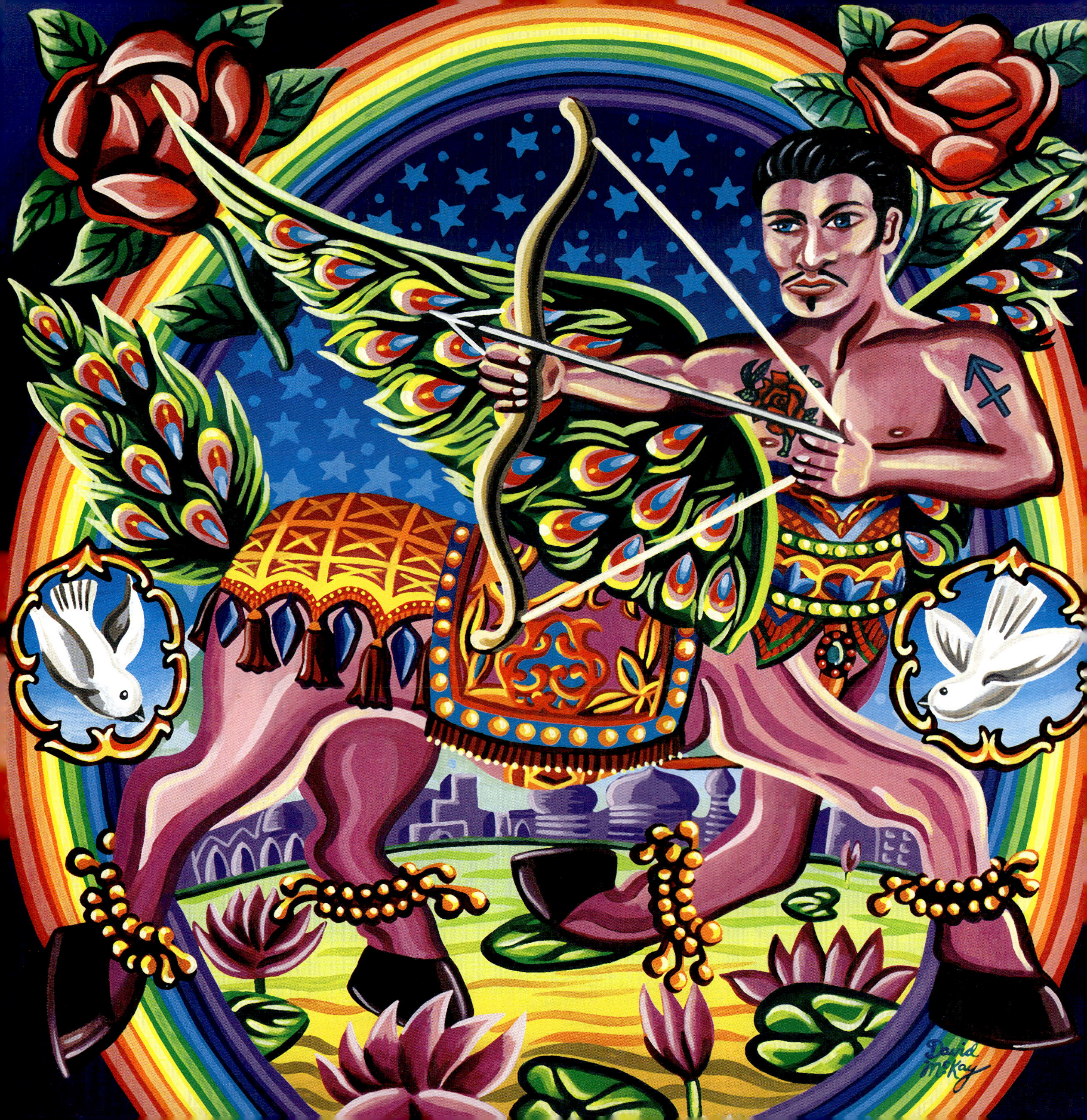
David McKay

sagittarius
a game affair

THE SAGITTARIUS APPETITE

Remember that crazy photo journalist character played by Dennis Hopper in Apocalypse Now? You know, the one dressed head to toe in political-activist khaki with about nine Pentax cameras strung around his neck, who kept babbling on about spiritual values and CIA conspiracy theories? Yeah him. Could be he was a Sagittarius. Earnest, passionate, and globally aware, Sagittarians are the explorer types. The kind who wear fly-fishing jackets and combat pants to go for a machiatto or leave a dinner party suddenly to disappear into an ashram for three months. OK, not all Sagittarians are old hippies and foreign correspondents, some transform their lust for life into evil empires [Rupert Murdoch] while others are lady-like hedonists [Betty Ford mother of the infamous celebrity detox clinic]. Either way, the zodiac buzz word here is 'expaaaaaand'. *What Sag wants out of food reflects what they want out of life - the big picture, colour and movement, second and then third helpings. Ruled by Jupiter, the god who protected Rome with a fistful of thunderbolts and symbolised by a centaur, Sag play the lofty philosopher one minute and the hungry horse the next.* While they earbash you about foreign policy, tend to their gamey tastes with roasted pigeon and roasted onions. Why roasted? Food prepared as close to the naked flame as possible keeps the edge alive for this fire sign. Accent your bird with the sweet spice of cinnamon ['Ah ... Morocco '67'] and nail them with fragrant comfort food like sweet potato mash with a whiff of ginger ['Maybe it was Prague']. Sagittarius will eat in the manner of the departing Amazonian explorer or the returning battleworn gladiator. In their eyes this is the fitting feast of champions but to anyone else, well, it's just plain greedy.

THE SAGITTARIUS SEDUCTION

Sagittarians do not want to get behind closed doors. In fact if you can take most of your doors off their hinges and replace them with beaded curtains or weathered-silk saris, all the better. Forget book ends, Tupperwear, message mugs, daggy snapshots of weddings and babies stuck to the fridge, laminex tables, and drawn Venetian blinds. Suburban confinement of any kind will kill the Sagittarian seduction. Build a wilder mood instead with sweeping views, the old Sag Sinatra singing *Come Fly With Me* and craggy relics from life's naked highway. Don't fear turning your house into a casbah with glittering purple Rajasthani cushions spread across Turkestan prayer rugs. Serve the wine in ultramarine blue Spanish goblets and flirt while casually leaning near an illuminated globe. As you let the music flit from Ukranian wedding songs to Zen flutes, serve the meal on top of an old steam trunk and light the scene with an oil lamp • If you have no flair for the exotic and simply cannot bring yourself to transform your house into a Community Aid Abroad boutique, decamp the lot and set it up on a cliff face near the ocean or in a field of dandelions • The menu for conversation must be rich with ethical arguments, the law, religion, politics and corn ball humour. It's all very second year university, isn't it? By dessert be prepared to discreetly look away when your guest goes for a fourth round of rhubarb icecream [they just love red fruits and sticky textures] then absent-mindedly begins to lick their plate. After-dinner games should include a blindfold and an atlas, poker or gin rummy and then, in the boudoir, perhaps a little pin the tail on the centaur •

cream of celery & asparagus soup with sesame biscuits **squab pigeon roasted on a bed of cinnamon & leeks** sweet potato & ginger mash **roasted onions with olives & thyme** rhubarb ice cream with warm caramelised apples

drinks a sauvignon blanc with the soup a spicy shiraz with the pigeon
a sweet semillon with the dessert

cream of celery & asparagus soup

1 bunch celery
1 litre chicken stock
1 leek, washed thoroughly
2 cloves garlic
1 teaspoon nutmeg
2 tablespoons butter
1 cup cream
2 peeled potatoes or 1 bulb celeriac
2 sprigs thyme
2 bay leaves
1 large bunch asparagus

SESAME BISCUITS
300 ml vegetable oil
1 tablespoon sesame seeds
1 tablespoon fennel seeds [aniseed]
150 ml white wine
2 tablespoons grated lemon zest
2 tablespoons grated orange zest
2 tablespoons grated fresh ginger
75 g sugar
450 g flour
1 teaspoon cinnamon
1/2 teaspoon ground cloves

SOUP
- Trim the asparagus - blanched tips will be used for garnishing the soup. Chop the stalks for the soup.
- In a large pot, melt the butter and sauté the leek, garlic and thyme before adding the chopped celery, asparagus stalks and celeriac or potatoes. Continue sautéing for another minute. Add chicken stock, bay leaves.
- Cook for approximately 25 minutes till the celeriac or potato is cooked.
- Remove from the heat and let cool slightly before passing it through the blender. Once puréed it will need to be sieved to remove the stringy bits from the asparagus.
- Cut the garnishing stalks of celery into fine jullienne strips and, with the asparagus tips, blanch quickly and refresh under cold water.
- Before serving return the soup to the saucepan and add the cream. Season well with the nutmeg. Heat and serve with garnish and sesame biscuits on the side.

SESAME BISCUITS
- Heat the oil in a saucepan. Put in the sesame seeds and aniseed. Put the seeds and the oil into a large bowl and beat in the wine, lemon and orange zest, ginger and sugar.
- Mix the flour into the spices and add to the rest of the mixture, adding a little water if it is too dry. Shape in a ball, wrap in cling film and rest for 30 minutes.
- Divide mixture into 20 balls. Flatten them on the baking tray and bake at 200°C for 15–20 minutes.

squab pigeon roasted on a bed of cinnamon & leeks

6 x 450 g baby pigeons [squab]
4 leeks, washed and cut into 5 cm pieces
6 sticks cinnamon
18 cloves garlic, peeled and kept whole
Peanut oil for rubbing the squabs' skin
Salt and pepper
1 large piece ginger, peeled and sliced very finely
3 star anise
1 tablespoon butter
2 tablespoons olive oil

SAUCE
200 ml white wine
100 ml kecap manis [sweet soy]
200–300 ml beef or chicken stock

TO PREPARE BIRDS
- With a sharp knife, trim off the wings and the heads [if still attached] of the birds. Place these in the oven to brown lightly before adding to the stock/sauce.
- Wipe out the insides of the birds and place 1 stick of cinnamon, 2 cloves of garlic, 1/2 star anise, a knob of butter, and some ginger, into each cavity.
- Set birds to one side while you prepare the leeks and the stock.
- Sweat off the leeks, and add to the remaining garlic and ginger in a small amount of olive oil and butter. Place the leeks into the bottom of a roasting pan and place the birds on top. The birds should fit in snugly together.

SAUCE
- Bring all the ingredients to the boil, including the wing tips and neck. Simmer for 10–15 minutes before straining.

TO COOK PIGEONS
- Preheat oven 240°C.
- Rub a little film of oil onto each pigeon and season well with salt and pepper.
- Pour 1/4 of the stock onto the leeks and place in the oven for 12–15 minutes. Once cooked, remove from oven and, with tongs, remove from the leeks. Set each pigeon to rest on a plate for up to 20 minutes [they will retain their heat well].
- While the birds are resting, strain off the leeks and set aside. Add the leek stock into a saucepan with the other stock and continue simmering. The birds will have created beautiful juices whilst cooking and these can be added to the stock simply by picking up each pigeon with tongs and, with the cavity facing downwards to the saucepan, letting the juices drain out.
- The leeks can be presented as a bed on which the pigeons will sit on each plate with the reduced sauce ladled over each bird.

sweet potato & ginger mash

850–900 g sweet potato [preferably kumara]
60 g butter
100 ml cream [approximately]
1 large piece ginger, grated
1/4 teaspoon fresh nutmeg
Salt and pepper

- Peel the kumara and chop into medium sized chunks. Cover with cold, salted water and boil with the ginger till the flesh is soft and ready for mashing. Drain well.
- While still hot and steaming, add the butter, nutmeg and cream. With a potato masher, mash the potatoes to a smooth, creamy consistency. You may need to adjust the quantity of cream depending on the kumara.
- This can be done in advance and warmed as necessary with the addition of a little more cream.

roasted onions with olives & thyme

200g baby pickling onions
1/2 bunch thyme
3 tablespoons olive oil
100g Kalamata olives
2 tablespoons balsamic vinegar
1 tablespoon brown sugar
Salt and pepper

- Peel the baby onions, leaving them whole. With the point of a knife, pierce them through to the middle, this will help them stay whole.
- In a baking tray, roll the onions around with the olive oil, thyme, brown sugar, salt and pepper. Place into an oven at 180°C and cook gently for 20 minutes.
- Now add the balsamic vinegar and increase the heat to 200°C for 10 minutes, gently turning the onions over after 5 minutes.
- Reduce heat to 180°C and add the olives, cooking for a further 5 minutes.

rhubarb ice cream with warm caramelised apples

1 tub very good quality vanilla ice cream
1 bunch rhubarb
Sugar
6 Granny Smiths
3 tablespoons honey
1 teaspoon ground cloves
1/2 teaspoon cinnamon
30 g chopped walnuts
30 g sultanas
3 tablespoons brown sugar
6 teaspoons butter
125 ml water

RHUBARB ICE CREAM
- Cut the rhubarb into 3 cm lengths discarding the leaves and the flat brown part at the bottom of the stalks.
- Soften the vanilla ice cream to a semi-frozen state.
- Place the rhubarb in a heavy bottomed saucepan [enamel, cast iron or stainless steel]. Sprinkle liberally with sugar and a couple of spoonfuls of water. Put the lid on and cook for around 5 minutes on medium heat.
- Remove lid and see how cooked the rhubarb is, it may need a couple more minutes. It should be very soft and mushy and easily broken up when moved around with a fork. Allow to cool.
- Once the rhubarb is cold, fold it through the vanilla ice cream and refreeze. It will take a couple of hours, so make sure you do this well in advance. The rhubarb can be cooked a couple of days ahead of time.

CARAMELISED APPLES
- Preheat oven 190°C
- Wash and wipe clean the apples, cut out the core and make a cut around the belly of the apple to stop them exploding.
- Combine the honey, brown sugar, cloves, sultanas, cinnamon and walnuts in bowl.
- Place the apples in a baking tray [with enough room so they don't quite touch] and spoon some of the honey and walnut mixture into each cavity. Dob each with butter.
- Pour approximately 125 ml water over them.
- Bake in the oven for 50–60 minutes occasionally basting the apples with the syrup that will be forming in the tray as they cook. [You may need to add extra water as they cook.]
- Serve warm with the rhubarb ice cream. The apples are best eaten straight from the oven rather than reheated.

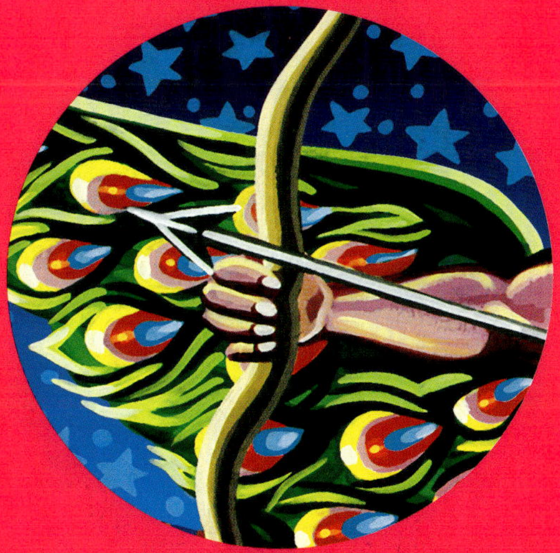

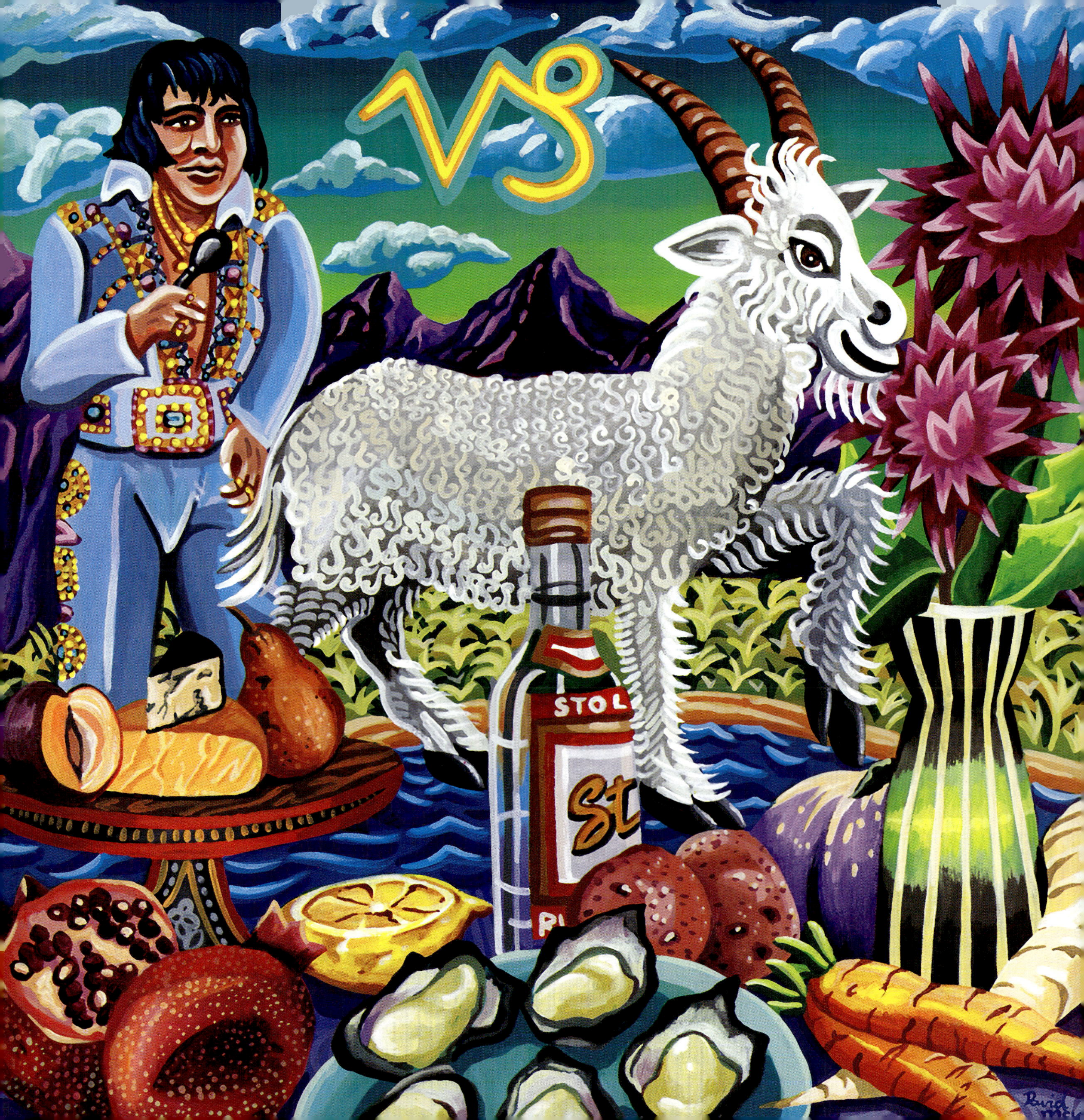
STOL

capricorn
traditional dinner

THE CAPRICORN APPETITE

There are two ways to eat a pomegranate. The first is to politely open the skin and scoop out the lush ruby fruit with a spoon. The second is to devour the fruit with bare hands, pressing the pulpy wet centre to your lips and letting the remainder trail down your front in a transport of sticky ecstasy. Capricorns prefer the Peter Greenaway version • The sensual key to Capricorn is duality. The goat might profess a taste for boarding school stodge, Jacobean tragedy and navy blue, but their secret life is one of ramapant sensuality. The aura of Saturn is one of melancholy, rigidity and order, but wed to that tacitern character is a craving for kicks. A subterranean desire to express a spark of creativity and release the primal howl that's being blocked by all that solid earth. To please a goat on an obvious level fill up the pantry with rare meats, dark fruits and berries, figs and quinces, fresh cheeses, antipasto and truffles. Overload their platter and forget flimsy, watery snacks • But to really make them love you, need you, and want to possess you, study the nuances of winter vegetables, seasoned wild game and decant rich red wine the colour of garnets. Imagine a dinner for a class of despotic royals who fancy themselves peasants and you have the makings of Capricorn's ideal feast - rustic and yet bloody posh to the core •

Few find the idea of a Saturday family lunch erotic but tradition turns Capricorn on. Wear silk garters beneath the table or reach across to graze her ankle with a straight face, as long as the table is set like a 17th century old master's still life and the centrepiece roast lamb is cooked with leeks and genius. Attracted to the signs of success that are lasting rather than nouveau, don't bother preparing some avant garde experimental salad for the goat. They prefer old ground explored with originality. The symbolic Capricorn food of seduction is the Jerusalem artichoke - hard on the outside, soft at the core, heavy on the palette with a lingering pungent aftertaste. Serve this icon of the sensual with the rich compliments of a potato and blue cheese torte, crisped prosciutto and marscapone on a rocket salad and then round off the mini banquet with a honey baked quince pizza. While Aquarius or Libra might feel swamped by such

THE CAPRICORN SEDUCTION

substantial fare, Capricorns simply view this spread as their due. Another clue for Saturnine success is bombast - slam this food down on the table with defiant flourish. If you make a mistake in the kitchen, make it look deliberate, purposeful, even! Capricorns are roused by authority and leadership. To set the mood, think of the hidden landscapes of dark mountains and tankstreams. Drawn to the deep, contemplative colours of the forest, Capricorns appreciate rich shades for the table setting - long thin branches strewn with deep-purple flowers, cut glass, a simple white table cloth, moss-coloured candles and the good linen, no paper napkins. It is also prudent to place a setting beneath their platter for as refined as goats are, once they start devouring the food they get earthy. Don't fuss over scraps or jumping up to stack the dishes. Attend instead to the discreet charm of the bourgeois. Capricorn seduction style is agile. Moving from the table to the chaise lounge with a lunge.

oysters with chilli, ginger & lemongrass sauce jerusalem artichoke & potato tortes layered with blue cheese, prosciutto & mascarpone, served on a salad of rocket, walnuts & peppered pear **leg of lamb stuffed with leeks & eggplant, roasted on a bed of wild garlic & celeriac** honey baked quince pizza with caramelised yoghurt

appetiser **vodka** entrée **chenin blanc** main **full-bodied cabernet sauvignon** dessert **a late-picked riesling**

drinks

oysters with a chilli, ginger & lemongrass sauce

Allow 4–6 oysters per person, leave on shell.

SAUCE
50 g white sugar
120 ml white vinegar
1 tablespoon kecap manis [sweet soy]
1 small piece ginger, grated finely
1 small chilli [seeds removed if preferred]
1 lemongrass bulb, smashed with back of knife and chopped very finely
2 cloves garlic, chopped finely
1/2 onion - sliced
120 ml water

- Place sugar and vinegar in a small, heavy bottomed saucepan, once sugar has dissolved place over high heat to caramelise [watch out for spitting caramel, it hurts!]. Remove from heat and add the water before returning to the heat once it has been absorbed. Add garlic, chilli, ginger, onion and lemongrass. Reduce heat and simmer for 20 minutes before adding the kecap manis. Remove from heat and allow to cool.
- Check over oysters for little bits of cracked shell and arrange on a platter. Place a teaspoon of sauce on each oyster before serving.

jerusalem artichoke & potato tortes with blue cheese, crisped prosciutto & mascarpone

TORTES
500 g Jerusalem artichokes
600 g potatoes, peeled
100 g butter [melted]
4 slices prosciutto
4 tablespoons mascarpone
50 g blue cheese [Lighthouse Blue, preferably]
Salt and pepper
2 sprigs fresh thyme, stalks removed
1 tablespoon olive oil
4 Teflon-coated individual torte tins with 2 cm straight sides

SALAD
2 ripe pears, peeled and quartered
1 bunch rocket, picked over and washed
100 g walnuts
100 ml extra virgin olive oil
25 ml balsamic vinegar
1 tablespoon Dijon mustard
Salt and pepper

- Very finely slice the potatoes and Jerusalem artichokes into rounds, place on kitchen towel to remove excess water and pat dry. Place in stainless-steel bowl and cover with the melted butter, salt and pepper to taste. Set aside.
- Gently heat 1 tablespoon of olive oil in frypan. When hot, quickly crisp the prosciutto and drain onto kitchen paper.
- Mix the blue cheese and mascarpone together with fresh thyme.
- Preheat oven to 200°C. Ensuring that the potatoes and Jerusalem artichokes are well coated in butter, use them to layer each tin in an overlapping fashion. On top of this first layer, spread the blue cheese mix, avoiding getting too close to the sides. Place prosciutto on top of mixture and then build up another layer of potato and Jerusalem artichoke, cheese mix and prosciutto and so on, until ingredients are used up, finishing with a layer of potato and artichoke on the top. Place in oven and cook for approximately 20 minutes.
- Meanwhile, slice pear finely and cover with olive oil, vinegar, mustard, salt and pepper, and toss gently. In a separate bowl, place the rocket and walnuts. Just before serving, add the peppered pear. Toss gently and arrange on plates just before the tortes come from the oven.
- Gently run a knife around the side of each tin and invert the torte onto a plate. With an egg slice, lift onto the salad and serve immediately.

leg of lamb stuffed with leeks & eggplant, roasted on a bed of wild garlic & celeriac

1 leg of lamb, ask butcher to remove the bone for you
1 large leek, trimmed of upper green part
1 small eggplant
6 sprigs fresh rosemary, stripped from stalk
1 large head of wild garlic
1 bulb celeriac
600 ml veal or beef stock
100ml red wine
100ml port
4 tablespoons olive oil
Chopped parsley, for garnish
Salt and pepper
String for tying lamb
Green beans for accompaniment

- Preheat oven to 250°C.
- Cut leek in half, lengthways and wash thoroughly to remove any grit. Plunge into boiling water for 45 seconds and rinse till cold, then pat dry.
- Cut eggplant lengthways into 1/16ths and salt. Leave for 20 minutes before rinsing and patting dry. Then gently brown the eggplant in the olive oil and leave to one side to cool.
- Peel and slice the celeriac and remove the outer husks from the garlic, leaving the cloves whole. They will soften and sweeten as they cook.
- To stuff lamb; place 6 pieces of string in parallel lines onto your work bench. Put the lamb down, skin side to the bench, across the string and season well with salt, pepper and half of the rosemary. Drizzle with olive oil and lie the leek and eggplant down the centre. Bring the sides of the lamb in, tucking in any extra flaps and try to make as firm a package as possible. Tie the strings securely.
- In a heavy bottomed baking dish, place the sliced celeriac and garlic. Put the lamb on top of this and pour over the stock, wine and port and then season the outer skin with salt and pepper and the remaining rosemary.
- After 20 minutes at 250°C, reduce the oven temperature to around 200°C and cook for a further 35 minutes. If you have an oven grill, brown the top of the lamb for a further 10–15 minutes, though this is not essential. Check that the celeriac is softened sufficiently, which will depend on the thinness of the slices. [These cooking times allow for the lamb to be pink. If you prefer it well done, simply extend the cooking time by 10 minutes.]

TO SERVE
Remove the string from the lamb. Place the celeriac and garlic onto a serving dish, pouring any extra liquid into a sauce boat. Slice the roasted lamb into 1 cm thick steaks and arrange on top of the celeriac. Sprinkle with parsley. Serve with green beans that have been tossed in extra virgin olive oil and with the sauce on the side.

honey baked quince pizza with caramelised yoghurt

HONEY BAKED QUINCE PIZZA
4 large quince
1 vanilla pod - slit
1 stick cinnamon
75 g white sugar
2 tablespoons honey
300 ml water
200 g puff pastry
1 lemon

CARAMELISED YOGURT
300 ml cream
100 g yoghurt
Brown sugar
Juice from one orange
6 ramekin pots, to serve the caramelised yoghurt

- Preheat oven to 200°C.
- Place the white sugar, honey, water, orange juice, vanilla, and cinnamon stick in a heavy bottomed sauce pan and bring to a rapid boil, then reduce the heat.
- Peel, core and slice the quince into 1/8ths, keeping them in acidulated water [i.e. with lemon juice added, to stop oxidisation].
- Add the quince to the gently boiling syrup and cover with a lid, leaving to simmer gently till slightly tender but by no means mushy. Remove from the heat and lift the quince pieces out with a slotted spoon and leave to one side to cool.
- Return the syrup to the flame and reduce further until it becomes thick and very syrupy.
- Roll out the puff pastry to a thickness of 4 mm. Using a plate, or a pastry cutter, cut into rounds of 12 cm. Place the pastry rounds onto a non-stick baking tray and gently arrange the quince pieces in an overlapping circle. Brush the quince generously with the reduced syrup and place in oven for 10–12 minutes.
- Serve with individual caramelised yoghurt pots on the side.

CARAMELISED YOGHURT
- Whip the cream till light and fluffy. Fold in the yoghurt and whip for a further few seconds, till yoghurt is fully combined. Spoon into separate ramekin pots and sprinkle liberally with brown sugar. Place in refrigerator for at least 2 hours before serving.

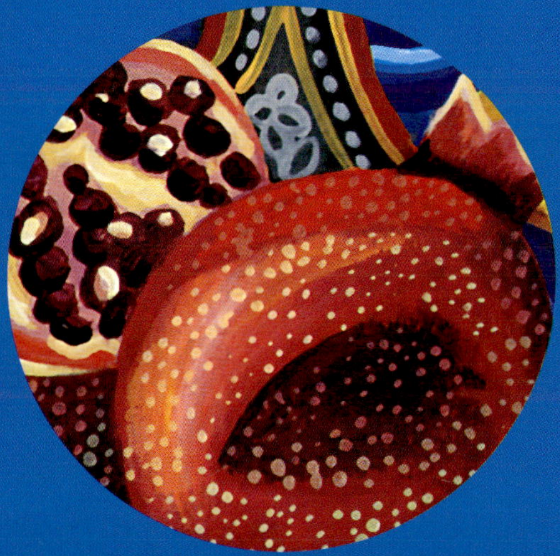

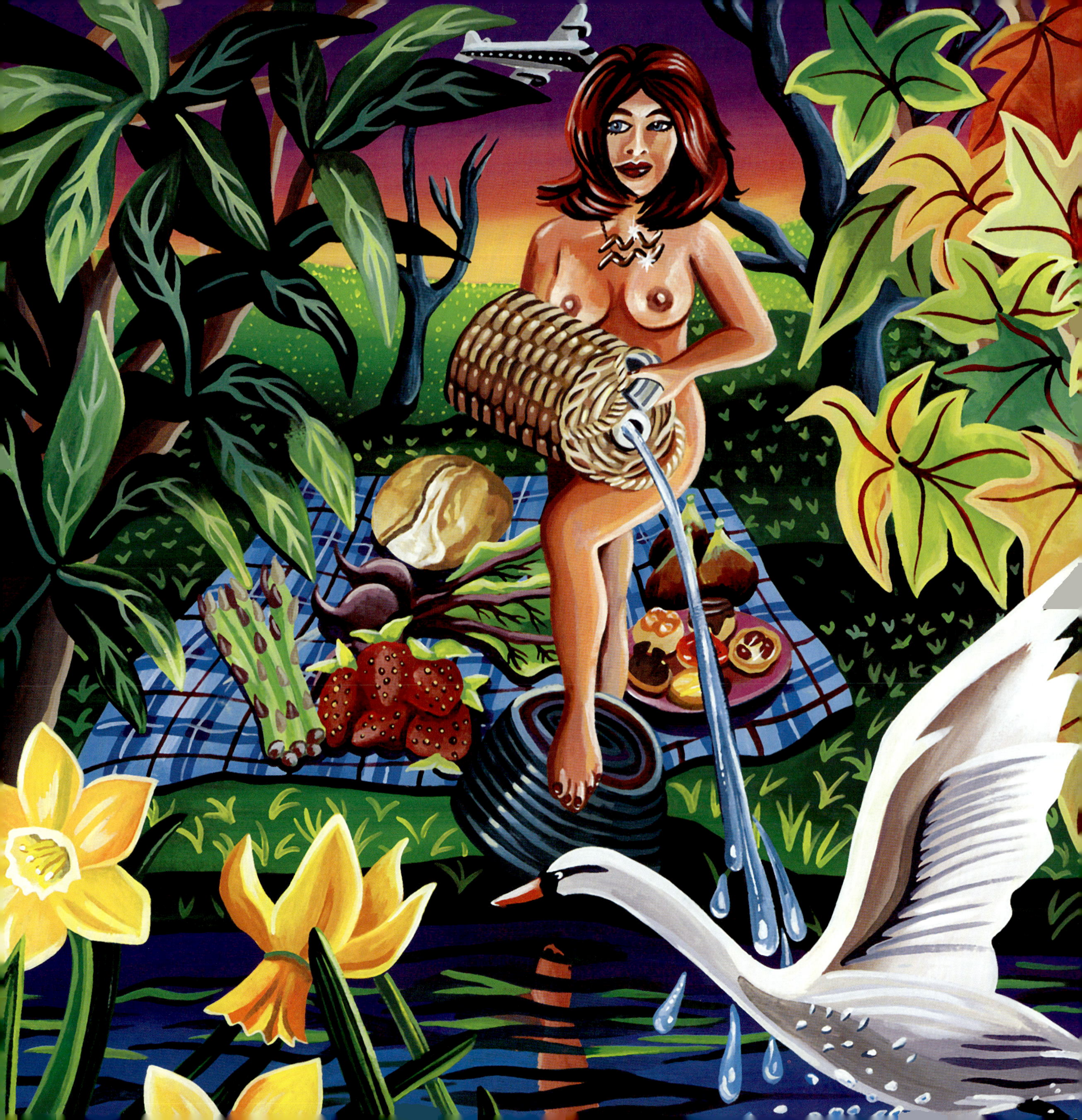

aquariusPICNIC

THE AQUARIUS APPETITE

There is no typical Aquarian taste sensibility because this is the sign of ultimate individuality. They like healthy food, they like gourmet food, they like bizarre combinations, and food made with high-tech equipment • Because it's impossible to bank on precisely what strikes their flighty fancy, a picnic is a good idea. Day or night. Whatever you do, don't dictate to an Aquarius - fixed menus, dinner at eight and tight table etiquette will only inspire these air signs to rebel and shock you. Some will act pregnant and demand chocolate and onions, others may drift from your banquet table with detached disinterest. Then there are the ones who will care more about the make of your new coffee machine than the macaroons you've sculpted with finesse • To avoid the inevitable disappointment that comes with trying to spoil an unpredictable Aquarian, choose food that is as mobile and eccentric as they are. The innovation of a crusty loaf stuffed with marinated antipasto will appeal to their saturnine tastes for simplicity. Their slightly sharp astringent palettes will also love the tang of asparagus in a fresh lime vinaigrette and the super healthy salad of spiced lentils. When the picnic basket is empty and the elderberry wine is on the roll, don't expect any compliments. The mind of the Aquarian darts around like Gemini but shrugs off easy charm. For these human lightning bolts food is just another weird texture in a world full of weird textures. Let them graze forever to the left of convention •

THE AQUARIUS SEDUCTION

A date at dusk at the observatory would be a good setting for an Aquarian picnic. Liberated by the vista of stars above their heads, any uncomfortable associations of home and hearth would be briskly swept away. It is asserted that Aquarians are the commitment phobes of the zodiac, anxious about intense emotion, repulsed by marital routine. I think entrapment was the term used by the last Aquarian I saw as he was disappearing into the side of an aeroplane. To seduce these evasive creatures you must never fret, overprepare or harry them. The key words to focus on instead are 'freedom' and 'invention'. A vague invitation: 'Maybe a picnic,' followed by a cool distracted greeting upon meeting: 'Oh, you came. Hello,' are effective ploys. Game playing? Perhaps. But sadly this is a case of fighting ice with ice. Lay out your morsels on an electric-blue cotton tablecloth strewn with daffodils, choose napkins the colour of sapphires and then abruptly stop fussing. Tend rather to the wild meanderings of your Aquarian's mind, even more bizarre turns of phrase and sudden frosty mood swings. Do not rush them back to your place or talk them into a corner, instead keep your mind focused on the broad expanse of starlit sky above you and the lofty concepts it evokes - science, the cosmos, UFOs, technology, the future. Big fat sweeping generalisations, polemical ethics and revolutionary philosophers are what the Aquarian feasts on. Spin them out far enough into that wild blue yonder and they'll rebound straight back into your arms - hungry, stimulated and electrically charged.

marinated antipasto in italian-style bread salad of spiced lentils & baby beetroot **asparagus with fresh lime vinaigrette** potato & mushroom salad with a light goat's cheese dressing **coconut macaroons** coconut syrup cake with strawberry cream & fresh figs elderberry wine or a chilled rosé drinks

marinated antipasto in italian-style bread

ANTIPASTO
Marinated eggplant
Red capsicum, washed
1 bunch English spinach, blanched
Artichoke halves
Roasted tomatoes
Olives
1 loaf woodfired Italian bread

VINAIGRETTE
1 teaspoon Dijon mustard
1 clove garlic, crushed
4 tablespoons extra virgin olive oil
1 tablespoon balsamic vinegar
1 dessertspoon capers, chopped
1 dessertspoon parsley, chopped

- Slice the Italian loaf in half lengthways. Remove most of the white soft bread. Drizzle the insides with some olive oil and season with salt and pepper. Layer up the vegetables in any order of preference, drizzling some of the vinaigrette between each layer as you go. Place the lid back on the bread and wrap the whole loaf very tightly in foil. The loaf can then be placed in the fridge and pressed down for a couple of hours.
- To serve, simply remove foil and cut into slices.

salad of spiced lentils & baby beetroot

500 g puy lentils, picked over for stones and rinsed under cold water
6 radishes, diced finely
2 tablespoons roasted pinenuts
2 tablespoons currants
2 tablespoons freshly chopped dill
2 tablespoons freshly chopped parsley
4 tablespoons olive oil
Juice of 1 1/2 lemons
Salt and pepper
1 teaspoon cumin seeds, toasted
1 bunch baby beetroot - cooked and cut in quarters
[one small can baby beetroots if fresh not available]

- Cover the lentils under cold water, bring to the boil and simmer gently for about 10 minutes. The lentils should remain firm; soft, but not mushy, to the touch. Drain well.
- Place all the other ingredients into a bowl and mix carefully, add the lentils, toss through thoroughly and transfer to storage bowl. Serve at room temperature.

asparagus with fresh lime vinaigrette

2 bunches fresh asparagus, blanched and refreshed under cold water
Juice of 2 limes
1 teaspoon Dijon mustard
3 tablespoons olive oil
1/4 teaspoon freshly grated ginger

- Make vinaigrette in a small jar and pour over the cold asparagus when ready to eat.

potato & mushroom salad with a light goat's cheese dressing

500g baby potatoes
125g mushrooms - sliced
125g green beans - cut into 2cm lengths
1 bunch chives
2 tbls olive oil
Salt & pepper

DRESSING
2 tbls plain yoghurt
2 tbls mayonnaise
1 - 2 tbls goat's cheese [according to taste]
Juice from 1/2 lemon

- Boil the potatoes and cut in half while still warm
- Blanch the green beans and mix with the potatoes and chopped chives
- Saute the mushrooms in the olive oil, season with salt and pepper and add to salad
- Mix all the dressing ingredients to a smooth consistency, add to the potato mix and coat the potato mixture
N.B A little extra goat cheese can be added to the salad if desired

coconut macaroons

MACAROONS
3 egg whites
150 g castor sugar
150 g desiccated coconut

- In a bowl over a saucepan of boiling water, whisk the egg whites and the sugar together until the sugar has been thoroughly dissolved [no longer than 3–4 minutes].
- Remove from heat and whisk in the coconut. Continue whisking for a further minute.
- Form small balls of mixture and bake at 180°C for about 5–8 minutes. When cooked and cooled, the biscuits should be crunchy on the outside and soft and chewy on the inside.
- Serve with fresh figs and strawberries.

coconut syrup cake with strawberry cream & fresh figs

140g butter
140g sugar
60g eggs
2 tbls golden syrup
1 cup desiccated coconut
1/2 cup milk
3/4 cup plain flour
3/4 cup desiccated self-raising flour
1 tsp. baking powder
2tbls mascarpone
[coconut syrup from Chinese food stores]
6 fresh ripe figs

- Cream the butter and sugar until fluffy
- Add the eggs one at a time, then add the golden syrup, macapone and coconut.
- Fold in the sifted flours alternately with milk
- Pour into prepared tin and bake for 40 minutes at 180c.

FRESH STRAWBERRY CREAM
5-10 large strawberries
150 ml cream
2 teaspoons icing sugar
2 drops vanilla essence

- With a fork gently mash stawberries
- Whip the cream with icing sugar and vanilla to firm peaks
- Fold in mashed stawberries - place in a bowl and refrigerate until needed
- Serve with the coconut syrup cake and fresh figs

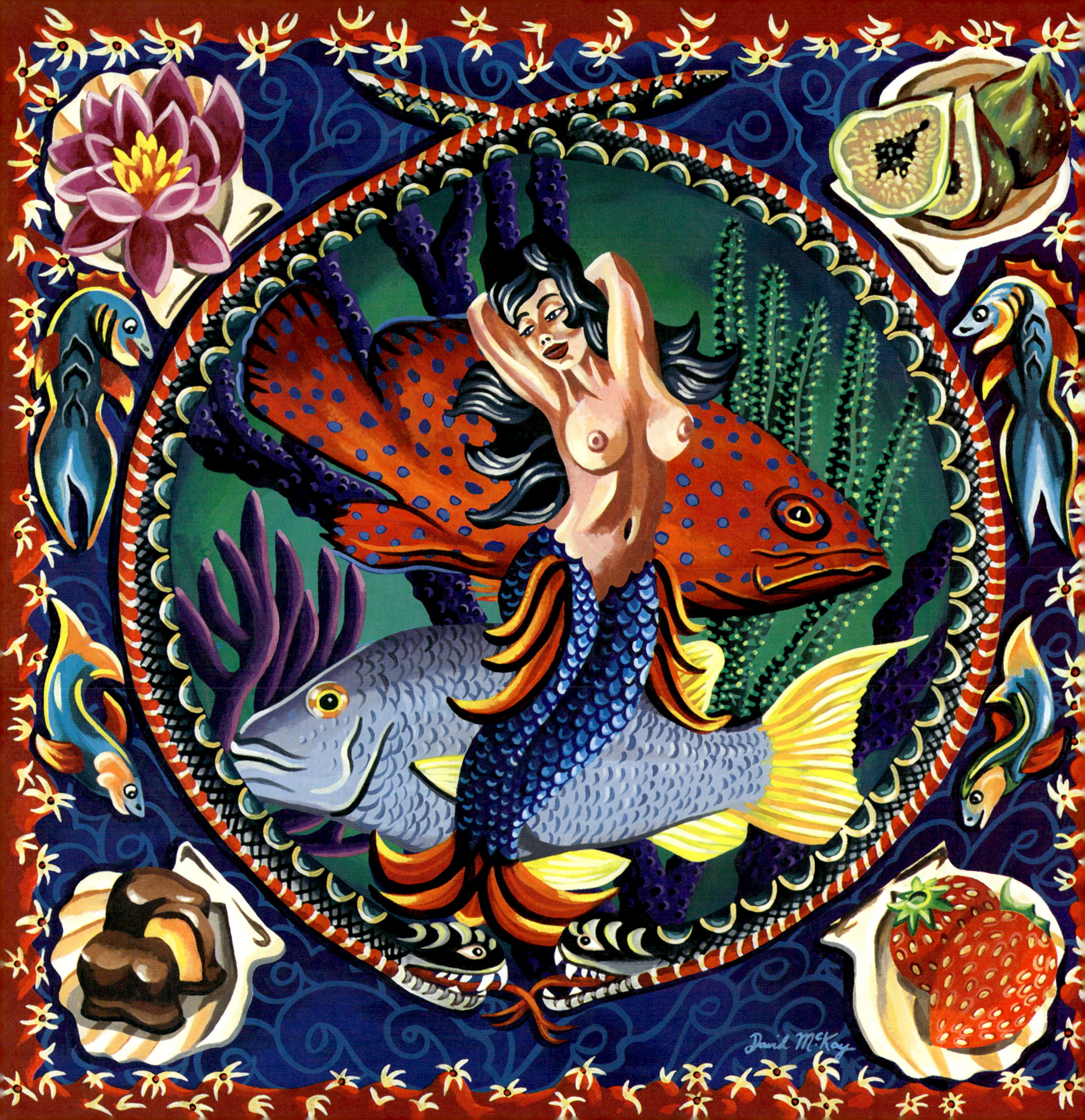
David McKay

pisce

MIDNIGHT FEAST

THE PISCES APPETITE

There is a legend that is useful in approaching the strange, passionate appetites of Pisces. The legend goes like this. In 1930 the Italian Futurist Filippo Tommaso Marinetti received a telegram from a broken hearted suicidal friend. To save him, Marinetti concocted a feast of 22 edible sculptures. There, in a villa by the edge of a lake, the desolate fellow feasted his eyes, then his tongue and his teeth, upon the flesh of timorous goddesses built from vanilla, sponge biscuits, chocolate, nougat and perfumed nectars. By dawn he was cured of his melancholy. Pure sensuality and a flight of uncensored fantasy had saved him. That doesn't mean that you have to rent a villa, cast your body in gelatine and build a lotus-petalled pathway to your bed chamber to win a fishy heart. No damn it, it's the spirit of the thing! Pisces respond to the waking dream, the absurd, the mystic. Like the ravaged lover in Marinetti's tale, to really move a child of Neptune you have to tend to the soul as well as the body. **The palette of the fish is not so far out. Of course they like seafood [trout, salmon, tuna, oysters], accented by brisk green tastes and the lush petals of an artichoke. They also quite fancy fruits and sugary tastes. Most of all they like a little drinky, a glittery pale challis of white wine or champagne that builds a fluid bridge between the real and the nebulous. To keep these super sensualists from floating downstream and out of your clutches forever, earth them. Crisp potato and cakes with quails' eggs provide a subtle blast of carbohydrate and protein, while asparagus spears wrapped in smoked salmon lend a savoury edge to the dreamy sweets Pisces devour. Yes, they take vitamins too.**

The midnight feast doesn't have to be held at midnight because, quite frankly, Piscean time frames are as floppy as Salvador Dali's melting alarm clocks. For this seduction whim is everything. Appear to whip these delicacies out of thin air, making it look like a flash of inspiration. Move your bed into the centre of the living room, suspend a fall of silver netting from the centre of the ceiling and light 30 aqua candles around the perimeter. Or place a vast glass bowl at the centre of the table ornamented by three floating lotus flowers and a single blue fish. Or serve the feast in a cave by the ocean or [more simply] drive your pick-up truck to the water's edge and dine seated on amethyst-coloured cushions laid out on the tin tray illuminated by scented

THE PISCES SEDUCTION

candles and blinking starlight [that one worked on me].
• However you dish it up, be as impractical as possible. Pisces have the logic of love poets. Oysters for breakfast, dessert for dinner, sex before conversation, love before honour and surrealist art movies running on a loop inside their heads. Think about that scene in Baz Luhrmann's Romeo and Juliet where Claire Danes ogles Leonardo De Caprio through the delicate shifting water of a tropical fish tank and then understand something important: Pisces see the whole world like that. Approach this romance with corny song lyrics, soothing tones of blue, unpredictable outbursts and a snorkel, all the while diplomatically steering your dreamers out of their tiny bubbles and into the lyrical pleasures of dry land •

asparagus spears wrapped in smoked salmon with horseradish & chervil cream fresh figs with venison prosciutto fresh oysters with a cucumber & dill salad crisp potato cakes with quail eggs & olive tapenade tiny rhubarb tartlets candied chestnuts dipped in chocolate a bowl full of succulent strawberries to be dipped in a glass of chilled champagne & fed into your lover's mouth

drinks   ice-cold champagne a lighter style late picked riesling
[the beauty of this midnight feast is that it can all be prepared well in advance of the actual occasion & placed onto a platter, refrigerated & later eaten as little bites of seductive temptation]

asparagus spears wrapped in smoked salmon with horseradish & chervil cream

1 bunch asparagus, about 8 spears
4 slices smoked salmon
3 tablespoons sour cream
2 teaspoons horseradish
1 dash white wine vinegar
Salt and pepper
3 stems chervil

- Combine the sour cream, horseradish, vinegar, salt and pepper in a bowl. Tear the leaves from the stalks of chervil, mix into the cream and chill.
- Trim the stringy ends off the asparagus [about an inch from the base] and blanch in boiling salted water until tender.
- Refresh the asparagus under cold running water and pat dry.
- Wrap each asparagus spear in half a slice of smoked salmon.
- When you are just about to serve the asparagus spoon the horseradish cream over the salmon and sprinkle with some more chopped chervil leaves.

fresh figs with venison prosciutto

4 ripe figs, choose figs that are almost splitting with succulent ripeness
8 very thin pieces of venison prosciutto [available from good delicatessens]
Extra virgin olive oil
Freshly cracked black pepper

- Cut figs into quarters.
- Gently roll the prosciutto around the figs.
- Arrange onto a platter and drizzle with extra virgin olive oil and cracked pepper just before serving.
N.B. If venison prosciutto is unavailable, substitute with Italian prosciutto.

fresh oysters with a cucumber & dill salad

Allow 3–4 oysters each
1 small Lebanese cucumber
2 sprigs dill
Salt and pepper
Balsamic vinegar

- Cut the cucumber into lengths, slicing as finely as possible. Sprinkle with the salt and pepper and leave for 10 minutes.
- Rinse the cucumber very well. Add the chopped dill and a touch of balsamic vinegar.
- Place a teaspoon of cucumber salad on the bottom of each oyster shell and top with the fresh oyster.

crispy potato cakes with quail eggs & olive tapenade

4 quail eggs

OLIVE TAPENADE
1 cup kalamata olives, stoned
1 tablespoon capers, chopped
2 anchovy fillets
1 clove garlic, minced
1/2 lemon, juiced
1 small handful basil leaves, chopped
1 small handful parsley, chopped
2 tablespoons olive oil
Black pepper
1 tablespoon red capsicum, finely diced
1 tablespoon tomato skin, finely chopped
2 teaspoons balsamic vinegar

CRISPY POTATO CAKES
2 large potatoes, peeled and grated
1/2 small onion, peeled and grated
1 egg, lightly beaten
Salt and pepper
3 tablespoons vegetable oil

QUAIL EGGS
• Put eggs in saucepan, cover with cold water and bring to boil - boil for 2–3 minutes.
• Refresh eggs under cold water, peel and cut in half lengthways.

OLIVE TAPENADE
• Chop the olives finely, mixing thoroughly with all the other ingredients in a bowl.
• Store in an airtight jar in the refrigerator covering the top of the tapenade with olive oil - it will stay fresh for weeks.

CRISPY POTATO CAKES
• Place the grated potato and onion in a clean tea towel and squeeze out all the excess juice.
• Mix in the egg, salt, pepper and 1 tablespoon of oil.
• Heat the remaining oil in a frypan and when it is very hot drop in heaped spoonfuls of the potato mixture and cook on both sides until golden and crispy.
• Place the cooked potato cakes onto a paper towel and drain off the excess oil.
N.B. These are better eaten warm, so if you are cooking them in advance reheat in the microwave or oven.

TO SERVE
• Warm the potato cakes and place a good dollop of tapenade on each one finishing each one with half a quail egg on top.

tiny rhubarb tartlets

6 tiny individual tart cases
1 bunch rhubarb, cleaned and trimmed
1 Granny Smith apple, peeled and grated
4 tablespoons raw sugar
4 tablespoons water
1 pinch ground ginger
1 pinch ground cinnamon
2 tablespoons double cream

• Cut the rhubarb into 11/2 cm pieces and place into a heavy based saucepan [preferably enamelled or stainless steel].
• Add all the other ingredients and cover tightly with a lid.
• Cook over a medium heat for about 5 minutes and give it a good stir - continue cooking if needed until rhubarb is totally mushy.
• Adjust sweetness according to taste.
• Once the mix is completely cool spoon a small amount of double cream into the bottom of each tart case and then top with the rhubarb.

candied chestnuts dipped in chocolate

250 g dark cooking chocolate
Candied chestnuts
[available from good speciality food stores]

• Melt the chocolate over a gently simmering bain-marie.
• Dip each chestnut into the chocolate and cover totally.
• Cover a plate in cling film and place the chocolate chestnuts on the plate in a cool place until the chocolate sets.

THE COSMIC FEAST glossary

ARIES March 21-April 20

planet Mars **element** Fire **colour** Red **tastes** Hot, Dry and Spicy
herbs & seasonings Cayenne Pepper, Garlic, Red Chillies [dried], Black and White Mustard seed, Basil, Vanilla, Peppermint
food stuffs Onions, Leeks, Hops, Pungent Foods. Red Foods - Meat [lamb, mutton, beef], Red Vegetables [Red Cabbage, Red Capsicum, Radishes, Red Onions], Red Fruits [Cranberries, Redcurrants, Rhubarb].
drinks Coffee, Lager, Beer and [of course] Red Wine
cooking methods Anywhere near a naked flame
flower Daisy, Honeysuckle, Thistle, Anemone
precious stone Diamond, Jasper
day of the week Tuesday
nutritional needs Aries governs the head and muscle tissue so the cell salt needed to repair nerves, muscles and grey matter is Potassium Phosphate. Potassium Phosphate foods are: Lettuce, Cauliflower, Olives, Cucumbers, Spinach, Radishes, Cabbage, Potatoes, Horseradish, Onions, Pumpkin, Lima Beans, Lentils, Walnuts and Apples
quirks Strident, confrontational, fiery, outdoorsy Aries types don't like parlour games or cool mushy foods. Aries tastes head south of the border.

TAURUS April 21 - May 21

planet Venus **element** Earth **colour** Pinks, Blues and Greens **tastes** Piquant, perfumed, aromatic
herbs & seasonings Coriander, Cloves, Parsley, Oregano, Peppermint, Vervain, Fenugreek Thyme
food stuffs Soft fruits:[Currants, Berries, Pears, Mangoes, Raisins Apricots, Bananas, Guavas, Lychees], White Meats and seafood served with fragrant marinades, Bread, Wheat and Oat based foods. Serve them Zucchinis and Green Capsicum but they go wild for the sweeter vegetables especially Sweet Corn, Cabbage, Artichokes and ginger
drinks Whisky, Rum and Rye
cooking methods Boiling, Poaching, the combining of warm and cool, for example, warm salads
flower Rose, Poppy, Foxglove, Daisy, Primula, Violet, Columbine
precious stone Emerald
day of the week Friday
nutritional needs Sulphate of Soda is the cell salt of Taurus, its mission is to control and regulate the supply of water in the body. Found most readily in Beetroot, Spinach, Horseradish, Cucumbers, Onions Pumpkin and.Coconut.
quirks Home and hearth, meadow and hayloft live at the sensual heart of Taurus appetites. Warm them, sweeten them and always replace novelty with solidity.

GEMINI May 22 - June 21

planet Mercury **element** Air **colour** Silver, Dove-Grey **tastes** Fragrant, Herby, Green, Gamey, Subtle and Bittersweet.
herbs Aniseed, Marjoram, Caraway, Balm
food stuffs Birds are the meat of Gemini: Chicken, Goose and Goose Liver, Duck and Turkey as well as Hare and Venison. Legume vegetables such as Peas, French Beans, Runner Beans, Haricot and Broad Beans. Nuts: Hazelnuts, Almonds, Walnuts and Coconuts. Fennel, Okra, Mushrooms and Carrots. Non-cereal seeds, Mulberries, Pomegranates
drinks Champagne and sparkling soft drinks
cooking methods Stir-fry, Microwave, Quick steam-the faster the better
flower Lavender, Lily of the Valley, Myrtle
precious stone Agate, Topaz
day of the week Wednesday
nutritional needs The cell salt of Gemini is Potassium Chloride which serves to regulate the fibrin of the blood and help these fast thinkers maintain clarity without burning out. Foods rich in Potassium Chloride are: Asparagus, Sweet Corn, Green Beans, Sprouts, Carrots, Cauliflower, Tomatoes, Celery, Oranges, Peaches, Pineapples, Apricots, Pears and Plums.
quirks Make it snappy, make it witty and don't weigh the quicksilver Gemini down. Think of the most elegant snack-food in the world and then serve with nonchalance.

CANCER June 22-July 23

planet Moon **element** Water **colour** White **tastes** Succulent, Fragrant, Dairy, Seafoods
herbs & seasonings Rosemary, Hyssop, Poppyseeds, Salt and Ginseng
food stuffs All Seafoods, especially shellfish [oysters, cockles, prawns, crabs and lobsters]. Caviar, Seaweed and Kelp. Dairy products: Cheeses, Cream, Milk, Yoghurts, Chocolate. Pale vegetables with a high water content: Cabbage, Cauliflower, Celery, Marrow, Melons, Watercress and Pumpkin, nuts and citrus
drinks White wine, Milk [not Goat's milk], Spring Water, Hot Chocolate
cooking methods Boiling, Poaching, Marinating and sometimes food served raw [like Sushi]
flower Waterlily, Poppy and White Rose
precious stone Pearl
day of the week Monday
nutritional needs Fluoride of Lime is the Cell Salt of Cancer. This cell salt attends to restoring the connective tissue in the body. Foods rich in Fluoride of Lime are: Egg Yolk, Whole Rye Flour, Cabbage, Lettuce, Watercress Pumpkin Potatoes
quirks The Moon Goddess that rules Cancer symbolises sensual abundance and fertility. Think of these buzz words: glowing, generous, rich. Leave the calorie counting to Virgo.

LEO July 24–August 23

planet Sun **element** Fire **colour** Gold and Scarlet **tastes** Spicy, Rich, Hot and Dry, Aromatic, Sweet and Sour
herbs Saffron, Turmeric, Cinnamon, Mustard, Ginger, Sage, Sunflower Seeds, Chamomile, Rosemary and Nutmeg
food stuffs Yellow and Orange coloured citrus fruits: Nectarines, Tangerines, Oranges, Lemons and Grapefruit. Orange Vegetables: Yams and Sweet Potatoes. Capon and Cockerel, the flesh of the heart. Sunflower Oil and Margarine. Gorgeous Curry flavours [see herbs] and Rice. As well as Cabbage, Eggplant and Mangoes
drinks Cider, Squash and Tea [but don't forget a good heavy red]
cooking methods Spit and Oven Roasting, Baking
flower Marigold, Peony, Sunflower
precious stone Ruby
day of the week Sunday
nutritional needs Leos need Phosphate of Magnesia to restore their nervous force and muscular vigour. This cell salt is richest in: Barley, Whole Wheat Bread, Rye, Almonds, Coconuts, Apples, Figs, Asparagus, Eggs, Cabbage, Cucumbers, Walnuts, Blueberries, Onions, Tomatoes, Coriander and Mint
quirks Serve them as royalty or don't serve them at all. Resplendent, Adventurous and Theatrical. The roaring MGM big cat is just a Leo waiting for dinner!

VIRGO August 24-September 23

planet Mercury **element** Earth **colour** Grey, Navy, White **tastes** Wholefood, Nutty Textures, Grains, Pure Flavours
herbs Basil, Cardamom, Caraway, Dill, Parsley, Vervain, Fenugreek, Liquorice, Marjoram
food stuffs *NOTE-Virgo is the wholefood vegetarian of the Zodiac. The ingredients listed here correspond with Gemini but their preparation should emphasize health rather than novelty. Vegetables grown under the earth like: Kohlrabi, Carrots, Potatoes and Celeriac. Above ground it's Mushrooms, Peas, Okra and all kinds of Beans: String, French, Haricot. Oats, nuts [Hazelnuts, Almonds, Coconuts].and rye The meat of all birds and Game birds. Fruits include Gooseberries, Loganberries, Mulberries and Pomegranates.
drinks Drinks that sparkle, champagne or the best naturally sparkling mineral water you can find.
cooking methods Steaming, Poaching or things served raw. Virgo likes clean food.
flower Brightly coloured small flowers such as Cat's Ear, Buttercup and Forget-Me-Not [see also the flowers of Gemini]
precious stone Onyx
day of the week Wednesday
nutritional needs Virgo diets need to tend to the processes of elimination through the skin and the liver. Potassium Sulphate helps cleanse the body. Foods rich in this cell salt are: Endive, Chicory, Carrot, Wheat, Oats & most salad vegetables
quirks These puritan souls like pure foods and they'll hector you to death to know the nutritional and fat content as well as the holistic properties of whatever they eat.

LIBRA September 24–October 23

planet Venus **element** Air **colour** Delicate Blues and Pinks **tastes** Perfumed, sweet smelling and delicately flavoured
herbs Mint, Cayenne, Thyme, Coriander, Fennel Seed, Dill, Parsley
food stuffs Venison, Veal, Beef, Goat, Chicken, Partridge, Pheasant, Lobster, Salmon and Sardines are all flesh foods ruled by Venus. Vegetables are Artichokes, Asparagus, Sorrel and Parsnips. Fruits are: Apples [for obvious biblical reasons], Currants, Oranges, Peaches, Apricots, Figs, Cherries, Grapes, Mangoes, Dates, Gooseberries, Strawberries and Raspberries. Wheat products of all kinds. Confectionery
drinks Sherry, Port and Sweet Liqueurs
cooking methods Boiling, Poaching, Steaming and Baking
flower Garden Roses, Bluebells
precious stone Sapphire, Jade
day of the week Friday
nutritional needs Librans need the cell salt of Sodium Phosphate to harmonise the balance between acids and alkalis. Sodium Phosphate foods are: Celery, Carrots, Spinach, Watercress, Asparagus, Beetroot, Peas, Yellow Corn, Apples Strawberries, Figs, Blackberries, Raisins, Almonds, Coconut, Oatmeal, Wheat and brown Rice
quirks These sweet-toothed romantics with impeccable taste know their way around a pastry shop and view icing sugar like the starlight of the Gods. Sneak in a few savoury elements but keep them fragrant.

SCORPIO October 24-November 22

planet Mars **element** Water **colour** Deepest Red, Black **tastes** Pungent, Spicy, Fermented [Mouldy and Curdled]

herbs & seasonings Chives, Rue, Chilli, Pepper, Tamarind, Basil, Cayenne Pepper, Garlic, Ginger, Mustard, Fish Pastes & sauce .

food stuffs Scorpio is associated with aquatic animals like Frogs and Snails. Foods that dwell in the underworld such as Truffles and fermented foods from Blue Cheese to Fish Sauce stir this palate. Mars plants are hot and come from hot climates: Capsicums, Nettles, Onion, Garlic, Radish, Leek and Eggplants. Mars meats are red but also include Shark and Goat. Mars also rules spiky skinned fruits like Pineapple, Lychees and the red skinned, tart tasting Rhubarb

drinks Tea, Coffee, Heavy Red Wine

cooking methods Marinating, Roasting, Spit Grilling, Scorching and Searing

flower Deep red flowers: Rhododendrons, Geraniums, Red Honeysuckle

precious stone Opal

day of the week Tuesday

nutritional needs Scorpio's cell salt is Sulphate of Lime which helps the blood clot and builds tissue. Foods rich in this cell salt are: Onions, Asparagus, Kale, Garlic, Mustard, Cress, Turnips, Figs, Cauliflower, Radishes, Leeks, Prunes, Black Cherries, Gooseberries, Blueberries and Coconuts.

quirks Passion, depth, intensity! Don't serve Scorpio a peanut butter sandwich. The recipes must be ancient, the intention must be concentrated and the flavour has to be as deep as a burning lake and as dark as a cave.

SAGITTARIUS November 23-December 22

planet Jupiter **element** Fire **colour** Purple, Deep Blue **tastes** Richly Fragrant, Sweet, Scented
herbs & seasonings Aniseed, Borage, Chevril, Cinnamon, Cloves, Nutmeg, Mint, Jasmine, Thyme, Sage, Sesame, Ginseng, Ginger, Sugar, Maple Syrup
food stuffs Jupiter meats are gamey: Venison, Pigeons, Antelope, Boar, Grouse, Quail and Pheasant. Vegetables include: Asparagus, Chicory, Endive, Leek, Turnip, Parsnips. Jupiter fruits are Bilberries, Figs and Limes. Added to this rather specialised list are Chestnuts, Olives, Rhubarb, Celery Onions and Dandelion flowers.
drinks Dandelion wine, Absinthe and Anisette liqueur
cooking methods Roasting, Steaming
flower Dandelion, Carnation
precious stone Amethyst
day of the week Thursday
nutritional needs Sagittarians need the cell salt of Silica which builds hair, skin and nails. Silica rich foods are the skins of fruit and vegetables and the outer coats or husks of all cereals.
quirks Sagittarius needs to feel they've travelled the world in their lunch hour so make your kitchen the United Nations of flavours. Collect recipes instead of postcards and throw all the doors and windows open, cage the centaur and they bolt. Forever.

CAPRICORN December 22-January 20

planet Saturn **element** Earth **colour** Forest Green, Navy **tastes** Sour, Bitter, Sharp, Savoury

herbs & seasonings Capers, Comfrey, Sage, Cumin, Knapweed

food stuffs Traditionally Capricorn is associated with winter foods, Christmassy flavours like Roast Turkey, Spit Roasted Goat, Lamb with Mint Sauce, Rich brown Gravies, Creamed Potatoes, Parsnip Soup, Puddings and Vegetables set in Gelatine or Marrow Jelly. Saturnine Vegetables are subterranean: Potatoes, Celeriac, Chicory, Salsify, Swedes, Radishes, Kohlrabi, Sea-Kale Beetroot, Artichokes and Eggplants. Barley, Goat's Milk, Malt, Starchy Foods and Quinces.

drinks Gin and Tonic, Aged Wines, Fortified Wines

cooking methods Roasts, Casseroles, Soups and Baking

flower Pansy

precious stone Turquoise

day of the week Saturday

nutritional needs Capricorns need Phosphate of Lime in their diet to settle the stomach and aid digestion. The foods richest in this cell salt are: Strawberries, Plums, Blueberries, Figs, Spinach, Asparagus, Lettuce, Cucumbers, Almonds, Coconut, Lentils, Brown Beans, Whole Wheat, Rye, Barley, Ocean Fish and Cow's Milk

quirks Pulsing beneath the solid composure of the Goat is a taste for the sensual. Boarding school tradition one minute, Roman orgy the next, that's the unpredictable element of Capricorn aesthetics.

AQUARIUS January 21-February 19

planet Uranus **element** Air **colour** Electric Blue **tastes** Gourmet eccentrics.- from Health Food to decadent Desserts
herbs & seasonings Cumin, Chillies, Pepper
food stuffs Whole foods: Beans, Seeds and Pulses. Game birds, Whole Grains, Subterranean Vegetables [see Capricorn]. Dark skinned fruits like Medlars and the Sloes
drinks Vodka
cooking methods Nothing set
flower Orchid
precious stone Aquamarine
day of the week Saturday
nutritional needs Aquarian diets need Sodium Chloride [salt] to balance the water levels in the body and to hydrate the system. The foods richest in this cell salt are: Strawberries, Apples, Figs, Spinach, Cabbage, Radish, Asparagus, Carrots, Cucumber, Lettuce, Celery, Chestnuts and Lentils.
quirks The quirks of Aquarius deserve their own book, in a series of volumes.
This is the sign of technology and invention so get out your 21st century pasta machine. At the same time Aquarius have a kink for nutrition and the logic of food so don't be surprised if they want weird and yucky combinations.

PISCES February 20-March 20

planet Neptune **element** Water **colour** Aqua Green **tastes**..Light, Watery, Aphrodisiac, Green, Salty
herbs Chicory, Lime, Mosses
food stuffs Obviously Seafood: Oysters, Trout, Salmon and Tuna. Watery vegetables: Cucumber, Lettuce, Cabbage, Spinach, Sprouts. Watery fruits: Honeydew melon, Watermelon, Grapes. Anything prepared with alcoholic marinades: preserved fruits, wine sauces, flambes, green flavours, liquid flavours, soups.
drinks Everything, but especially White Wines and Champagne
cooking methods Steaming
flower Waterlily
precious stone Moonstone
day of the week Thursday
nutritional needs The cell salt crucial to Pisces is Phosphate of Iron. Iron rich foods are Spinach, Lentils, Cabbage, Onions, Barley, Lettuce, Strawberries, Radishes and Pumpkin.
quirks Flighty Mermaids and sons of the Ebb-tide need earthing. Add some earth vegetables to their seafood platters and a dollop of heavier stewed fruits to their Champagne sorbets. The foods that govern Pisces are not always the foods that Pisces needs. Man cannot live on oysters and champagne alone but Pisces will try!

index

aioli, 80
almonds
    coconut and almond syrup cake, 62
antipasto, marinated, in Italian-style bread, 107
apples, caramelised, 90
apricots
    spicy tomato and apricot chutney, 27
Aquarius, 102-9, 129
Aries, 4-13, 119
artichokes *see* Jerusalem artichokes
asparagus
    with black mustard seeds and cinnamon, 47
    cream of celery and asparagus soup, 87
    with fresh lime vinaigrette, 108
    spears wrapped in smoked salmon with
        horseradish and chervil cream, 115
avocado dressing, 11

baked beans with roasted tomato and basil, 58
balmain bugs
    Catalan casserole of chicken, balmain bugs,
        prawns and squid, 38
Balmoral biscuits, 70
banana chillies, sweet, barbecued with sour
  cream, coriander and chives, 12
barley and coriander cakes with mango
  chutney and spiced cucumber raita, 45
beans, haricot
    baked beans with roasted tomato and basil, 58
beef brisket with red braised sauce and
  spinach, 20
beetroot
    salad of spiced lentils and baby beetroot, 107

biscuits
    Balmoral, 70
    sesame, 87
blackberries
    raspberry and blackberry compote, 72
bloody Mary, 63
bread, raisin naan, 48

cabbage
    chilli roasted chicken with deep-fried cabbage
        and spring onion, 20
    with onion, fennel and ginger, 47
cakes
    barley and coriander, 45
    crispy potato, 116
    parsnip and potato, 37
    see also syrup cake
Cancer, 32-9, 122
Capricorn, 92-101, 128
capsicum
    chilled red capsicum and tomato soup with
        fresh prawns, 79
caramelised apples, 90
caramelised yoghurt, 100
Catalan casserole of chicken, balmain bugs,
  prawns and squid, 38
celeriac and smoked salmon remoulade served
  on garlic croûtes, 28
celery
    celery, almond and cream cheese
        sandwiches, 69
    cream of celery and asparagus soup, 87
cheese and spring onion quesadillas, 9

cheesecake, Majorcan style citrus and honey, 39
chestnuts, candied, dipped in chocolate, 117
chicken
    Catalan casserole of chicken, balmain
      bugs, prawns and squid, 38
    chilli roasted, with deep-fried cabbage and
      spring onion, 20
    marinated, with a spicy tomato and apricot
      chutney, 27
    mushroom caps filled with chicken and
      marjoram, 60
    Pablo's chicken with potatoes and aioli, 80
    and watercress sandwiches, 69
    chicken liver mousse with warm toast, 31
chilli, ginger and lemongrass sauce, 97
chocolate
    candied chestnuts dipped in chocolate, 117
chutney, spicy tomato and apricot, 27
citrus and honey cheesecake, Majorcan
  style, 39
coconut
    coconut and almond syrup cake with fresh
      mango salad, 62
    coconut cream, 49
    coconut crunchies, 81
    coconut macaroons, 109
    coconut syrup cake, 109
coconut milk
    ginger and coconut milk custards with
      fresh mango salad, 21
coffee
    cremat, 39
    spiced, 13

compote
    fig, 71
    raspberry and blackberry, 72
coriander
    barley and coriander cakes with mango
      chutney and spiced cucumber raita, 45
cremat, 39
crudités with a spinach, hazelnut and olive oil
  dipping sauce, 28
cucumber
    and dill salad, 115
    fennel and cucumber salad with dill
      mayonnaise, 61
    sandwiches, 69
    spiced cucumber raita, 45
curry, sweet potato and apple, 46
custards, ginger and coconut milk, with fresh
  mango salad, 21

dill
    cucumber and dill salad, 115
    fennel and cucumber salad with dill
      mayonnaise, 61
    fennel seed and dill mayonnaise, 27
dipping sauce
    soy, 29
    spinach, hazelnut and olive oil, 28
    sweet chilli and cucumber, 19
dressing
    avocado, 11
    light goat's cheese, 108
duck livers, grilled, served with parsley and hazelnut
  pesto on whole-wheat pancakes, 59

eggplant
    lamb leg stuffed with leeks and eggplant, roasted on a bed of wild garlic and celeriac, 99

fennel and cucumber salad with dill mayonnaise, 61
fennel seed and dill mayonnaise, 27
figs
    fig compote, 71
    fig shortbreads, 71
    fresh, with venison prosciutto, 115
    spiced, with coconut cream, 49

Gemini, 22-31, 121
gimlet, classic, 51
ginger and coconut milk custards with fresh mango salad, 21
goat's cheese dressing, 108
guavas, fresh, poached in cinnamon and vanilla, 13

hazelnuts
    parsley and hazelnut pesto, 59
    spinach, hazelnut and olive oil dipping sauce, 28
honey baked quince pizza with caramelised yoghurt, 100

ice cream, rhubarb, 90

Jerusalem artichoke and potato tortes with blue cheese, crisped prosciutto and mascarpone, 98

kumara, 89

lamb
    leg stuffed with leeks and eggplant, roasted on a bed of wild garlic and celeriac, 99
    marinated barbecued leg, 10
    marinated lamb racks with sweet potato and apple curry, 46
lassi, 51
leeks
    leg of lamb stuffed with leeks and eggplant, roasted on a bed of wild garlic and celeriac, 99
    squab pigeons roasted on a bed of cinnamon and leeks, 88
lemon syrup, 62
lentils
    salad of spiced lentils and baby beetroot, 107
    spiced lentil and spinach salad, 12
Leo, 40-51, 123
Libra, 64-73, 125
lime and peach wine spritzers, 63
lobster and fresh mixed fungi salad with egg noodles, 19

macaroons, coconut, 109
mango salad, fresh, 62
mar i muntanya, 38
mayonnaise, fennel seed and dill, 27
muesli, fresh apple and pear, 57
mushrooms
    lobster and fresh mixed fungi salad with egg noodles, 19
    mushroom, rosemary and almond palmiers, 30
    mushroom caps filled with chicken and marjoram, 60

potato and mushroom salad with a light goat's cheese dressing, 108

naan bread, raisin, 48
noodles, egg
    lobster and fresh mixed fungi salad with egg noodles, 19
nougat
    prune and vanilla, served with coconut crunchies, 81

olive tapenade, 116
onions, roasted with olives and thyme, 89
oysters
    with a chilli, ginger and lemongrass sauce, 97
    fresh, with a cucumber and dill salad, 115

palmiers, mushroom, rosemary and almond, 30
pancakes, whole-wheat, 59
parsley and hazelnut pesto, 59
parsnip and potato cakes, 37
peaches
    glazed peach tartlets, 70
    lime and peach wine spritzers, 63
pesto, parsley and hazelnut, 59
picada, 38
pigeons, squab, roasted on a bed of cinnamon and leeks, 88
pilaf, roasted almond and saffron rice, 50
pimms with cucumber, orange, strawberries and borage, 73
Pisces, 110-17, 130

pizza
    honey baked quince pizza with caramelised yoghurt, 100
potatoes
    crispy potato cakes with quail eggs and olive tapenade, 116
    parsnip and potato cakes, 37
    potato and mushroom salad with a light goat's cheese dressing, 108
    roasted, with avocado dressing, 11
prawns
    Catalan casserole of chicken, balmain bugs, prawns and squid, 38
    chilled red capsicum and tomato soup with fresh prawns, 79
    deep fried prawn balls with a sweet chilli and cucumber dipping sauce, 19
    fresh prawns with a fennel seed and dill mayonnaise, 27
prune and vanilla nougat served with coconut crunchies, 81
pumpkin, chillied, with walnuts wrapped in corn husks, 11

quail eggs
    crispy potato cakes with quail eggs and olive tapenade, 116
quesadillas, cheese and spring onion, 9
quince
    honey baked quince pizza with caramelised yoghurt, 100

raisin naan bread, 48
raspberry and blackberry compote, 72
rhubarb
    rhubarb ice cream with warm caramelised apples, 90
    tiny rhubarb tartlets, 117
rice
    roasted almond and saffron rice pilaf, 50

Sagittarius, 82-91, 127
salad
    cucumber and dill, 115
    fennel and cucumber, with dill mayonnaise, 61
    lobster and fresh mixed fungi with egg noodles, 19
    pear, rocket and walnut, 98
    potato and mushroom, with a light goat's cheese dressing, 108
    spiced lentil and spinach, 12
    of spiced lentils and baby beetroot, 107

salmon, smoked
    asparagus spears wrapped in smoked salmon with horseradish and chervil cream, 115
    celeriac and smoked salmon remoulade served on garlic croûtes, 28
    toasted rye bread with smoked salmon and a fennel and cucumber salad, 61
salsa, watercress and shallot, 37
sandwiches, finger, 69
sangria mexicana, 13
sardines, grilled, on crisped parsnip and potato cakes with watercress and shallot salsa, 37
sauce, chilli, ginger and lemongrass, 97

sauce, dipping *see* dipping sauce
scones, warm, served with raspberry and blackberry compote and mascarpone, 72
Scorpio, 74-81, 126
sea and mountain, 38
sesame biscuits, 87
shortbread
    fig, 71
    Indian, 50
smoked salmon
    asparagus spears wrapped in smoked salmon with horseradish and chervil cream, 115
    celeriac and smoked salmon remoulade served on garlic croûtes, 28
    toasted rye bread with smoked salmon and a fennel and cucumber salad, 61
soup
    chilled red capsicum and tomato, with fresh prawns, 79
    cream of celery and asparagus, 87
spinach
    beef brisket with red braised sauce and spinach, 20
    spiced lentil and spinach salad, 12
    spinach, hazelnut and olive oil dipping sauce, 28
spritzers, lime and peach wine, 63
squab pigeon roasted on a bed of cinnamon and leeks, 88
squid
    Catalan casserole of chicken, balmain bugs, prawns and squid, 38
    stuffed with black rice, 79

strawberries
    fresh strawberrry cream, 109
sweet potato
    and apple curry, 46
    and ginger mash, 89
syrup cake
    coconut, 109
    coconut and almond, 62

tapenade, olive, 116
tartlets
    glazed peach, 70
    tiny rhubarb, 117
Taurus, 14-21, 120
tequilla shooters with spicy chasers, 13
toasted rye bread with smoked salmon and a fennel
  and cucumber salad and dill mayonnaise, 61
tomatoes
    chilled red capsicum and tomato soup with
      fresh prawns, 79
    roasted, 58
    spicy tomato and apricot chutney, 27
tortes, Jerusalem artichoke and potato, 98

vegetable rolls in rice paper with dipping sauce, 29
venison prosciutto, fresh figs with, 115
vinaigrette, 107
    fresh lime, 108
Virgo, 52-63, 124

watercress and shallot salsa, 37

yoghurt, caramelised, 100